KILLING KYLE ORTH

KYLE R. HUNTER

KILLING KYLE ORTH

The Death of a Criminal & Life of a New Man

KYLE R. HUNTER

For more information, visit: killingkyleorth.com
ISBN: 979-8-9946995-0-8 (hardcover)
ISBN: 979-8-9946995-1-5 (paperback)
ISBN: 979-8-9946995-2-2 (eBook)

Library of Congress Control Number: 2026902673

Edited by Teeg Stouffer
with Amy Stouffer, Kelsey Moore, Donna Lunstrum,
Wendie Pecharsky and Michelle Hill

Cover Art by Nick Johnson
Cover Design by Nydia S. Robles
Interior Design by Amit Dey

TABLE OF CONTENTS

ACKNOWLEDGEMENTS

On the surface, *Killing Kyle Orth* sounds like a story about a drug addict who found redemption through God. It is that, and I am grateful. But this book is also something deeper. It is the story of a community of believers who stood in the gap for me when I could not stand on my own.

To Bart Woods, my mentor and spiritual father, thank you for pouring out your life for mine. Thank you also to Jenny, for opening your heart and your home every time Bart brought me through the door. You welcomed me into your family on more occasions than anyone should have had to, and you did it with grace.

To Betty Criddle, my spiritual mother, thank you for loving a "load" like me. You saw past the wreckage and insisted there was still something worth fighting for.

To Kevin and Aroea Knox, thank you for standing in the trenches for my marriage. You fought alongside us when it felt like everything was slipping away.

To Travis and Christy Kolder, thank you for showing me what it truly means to love your neighbor. Your kindness arrived right when I needed it.

To Matt and Cindy Walker, thank you for inviting me into your home and giving me a place to stay when I had nowhere else to land.

To Ron Ziegler, thank you for second chances, for trusting me to be a Development Director, and for showing me what "honorable" looks like in the flesh. You set a standard that I still chase.

To Mike Johnson, a coach to coaches, thank you for guiding me and for being a friend who spoke truth with compassion.

To Brad Singleton, thank you for pushing me to grow, for visiting me in prison, for opening your home to me, and for believing in my potential long before I had the courage to see it.

To Paul Phelan, thank you for inviting me into your Bible study and for the many men in that room who helped shape my theology over the last five years. Your group became a forge, and I am being refined there.

To Pete and Suzy Lammers, thank you for believing in me to lead. You gave me opportunities that reshaped my future.

To Lavonne Johnson, thank you for counseling me and countless others. Your steady presence carried me through storms I could never have navigated alone.

To my wife's family, thank you for accepting me and giving me a place at your table. You became the family I prayed for when I had none.

To Gary Krogmann, thank you for sitting on the steps with me when my world felt like it was falling apart. Your quiet presence said more than any speech ever could.

To Teeg Stouffer, thank you for believing in this project and for standing with me as a friend. You saw a story worth telling even when I struggled to believe it myself.

To my daughters, you are the bright threads that hold my heart together. You are proof that God gives beauty for ashes.

And to my beautiful wife, Dawn, thank you for choosing to stand by me in sickness and in health, in confusion and in clarity, in the moments when hope felt close and in the moments when it felt impossibly far. Thank you for listening for God's voice, for believing in the calling over your life, and for reminding me of mine when I forget it. Your faithfulness has been one of the clearest evidence of grace I have ever known.

Every name here (and so many more that I fail to mention) represents a miracle. Together, you stitched hope back into a life that had unraveled. This book is not just about the death of the old Kyle. It is about the community who breathed life into the man I am becoming.

Thank you for loving me through the process. Thank you for proving that redemption is rarely a solo journey.

FOREWORD

There are stories that entertain, stories that inform, and then there are stories that confront a person by holding up a mirror to the darkest and brightest corners of the human heart. *Killing Kyle Orth* is one of those stories. It is raw, unvarnished truth, pulled from the grit and gravel of a life most people only see in headlines or hear about in whispered conversations. Yet it is also a story soaked in hope. Not the thin, fragile kind that depends on circumstances, but the kind that has weight to it. The kind that survives prison cells, hotel rooms, addiction, relapse, betrayal, and the quiet ache of loneliness that follows a person long after everyone stops loving them.

On the surface, this book is about a hopeless drug addict who somehow found his way home. That alone would be enough for most memoirs. But this one is different. This is not just a redemption story; it is a resurrection story. It is about a man who had to die before he could ever learn how to live. It is about killing the old self, the broken self, the self that kept dragging him into chaos. It is about watching that version fall away layer by layer until only a tender, humbled, Spirit-rebuilt man remains.

But the heartbeat of this book is something even deeper. It is the story of a community of believers who refused to give up on someone everyone else had already buried. People who stood in the gap when he could not stand on his own. People who carried him when he could not walk. People who did the hard, uncomfortable, time-consuming work of being the hands and feet of Jesus, not in a polished church setting but in living rooms, courtrooms, jail visits, hospital beds, and late-night phone calls.

Mentors who became fathers. Women who became mothers. Friends who became brothers. Pastors and families who opened their homes. A wife who chose covenant over comfort. A Savior who reached deeper than shame could go.

This book does not hide the mess. It does not soften the blow. It honors the truth that recovery is rarely a straight line, faith is often forged in relapses and restarts, and transformation usually happens through people loving someone long before it happens inside the person whom they love. It reminds the reader that miracles often look like ordinary people stepping into extraordinary obedience.

Kill the old self, let Christ raise a new one. That is the theme echoing through every chapter. Not because it is a clever idea, but because it is the only thing that ever worked.

If you are holding this book, prepare yourself. Parts of it will sting. Parts will make you shake your head. Parts will break your heart. And parts will fill you with gratitude for the God who still rescues, still restores, and still rebuilds what seems beyond repair.

More than anything, this book is a reminder that no one is too far gone, no story is too tangled, and no past is too heavy for the One who specializes in bringing dead things back to life. The man you are about to meet is proof.

Welcome to *Killing Kyle Orth*. May it stir something deep inside you, and may it remind you that the hardest soil often produces the strongest roots.

Bart Woods

PUBLISHER'S NOTE

I have a front row seat for this story. It comes not just from being the book publisher, but by being in Kyle's closest circle – we spend *a lot* of time together.

In light of that, I think it bears stating that the author – my friend – is not without his faults. Nor am I. Nor are you. But he has my trust and my confidence because I know his heart is oriented toward Jesus. It's from that deep trust that I have been not just willing, but eager to partner with him on this book and the film of the same name.

It's been my privilege and honor.

As a content editor for the book, I'll tell you up front: Some of the names have been changed and some of the locations and details have been blended together. There's a line in the Bible, "And there are also many other things which Jesus did, that if they should be written every one, I suppose that even the world itself could not contain the books that could be written." Well, the same might be said of Kyle, but the stories about him would not be as wonderful as the ones that would be written about Jesus. To get the message of this book – even to get a clear picture – you really don't need every last story, every last detail. But you do need honesty, and this has been written honestly, even though some parts have been deliberately omitted or combined for clarity and out of respect.

A few people might also push back on the subject of the book, and in the process of this project I've met some of them. They say things like, "people don't change … a leopard doesn't change its spots." That sort of idea … it's rooted in past hurts, but not necessarily present reality. When someone says something like that, what they're really saying is, "*I choose* not to trust this person," which is different from "*that person* can't…"

Sometimes people don't believe a person can change, or has changed, because *we* haven't changed. Or maybe it's because we don't want them to. It screws up our narrative.

But we really don't get to determine what other people can or can't do when it comes to these things … but God does. And that's good news, because He's the one who can transform us. In fact, he brings people who were dead in sin to life – he can raise us to totally new lives.

I know this personally, because God did this for me, too.

And it's especially easy for me to believe in the case of my friend, because I've been right here, witnessing it in real time with my own eyes.

So what you're about to read is not a fictionalized version of the events, just an abridged one. It's the story of how a little boy, full of potential, turned into a violent criminal and then … the story changed in ways nobody expected.

I'm interested in what you and God decide to do with your story, too. I hope this one gives you inspiration! Who knows? Maybe someday I'll get a chance to help you tell yours.

Teeg Stouffer

The sound of bullets punching through metal
sounds different in real life than it does in a movie.

The gunshot itself seems both far off and deafening,
and by the time the bullets strike you,
you're already in shock;
the world is in slow motion, sounds are kind of
like how they are when you're under water.

The glass that rains on you,
the screech and thud of every new bullet,
your own blood,
the flashes from the muzzle of the guns in the night,
they're so different in real life than in a video game.

You smell them.

1
MEET KYLE ORTH

Finally, the shots stop. Twenty-six in all. My stunned silence. Scenes from my life flash before my eyes. Then I hear yelling: "Put your hands up! Get out of the car!"

I open the car door and fall to the ground. Two officers drag me over rough pavement toward their patrol car, my knees scraping, my body limp, bleeding.

The action around me zooms out and then quickly back, distorted, disoriented, spinning. What is happening to me? Where am I? Who…?

They say what I haven't realized yet: I've been shot. Three times.

Panic floods my mind. The cold wash of terror and shock washes over my entire body. A black puddle glimmers red in the streetlight, blood filling the dirty pothole I am dying in as I fade away.

All I can think about is how I have failed, how I failed everyone.

Failed myself.

Raging failure.

They know my name.

Kyle Orth.

And I am dying.

2

DYING TWICE

I hated myself, my life, this mess. I cursed, slurring and sputtering all kinds of profanities. Would these be my last words? I drifted in and out of consciousness after that. The red and blue lights on the ambulance faded to black, and I began to travel to a different world. The sound of those gunshots that had been echoing in my head went silent and I finally blacked out completely.

Nurses burst through the doors of the emergency room to the ambulance. They pushed the gurney with my lifeless body into the operating room. I heard whispers, smelled antiseptic and cleaning products, and then I was out again, this time under the care of an anesthesiologist and a surgeon. I made it through surgery. As I came to, I tried to move my hand to my face but I couldn't. Restraints. I was a prisoner.

Opening my eyes took every ounce of my strength, but when I finally did, I saw that I was surrounded by a roomful of cops. Immediately, I felt regret. Why hadn't I died in that alley? I had questions but lacked the strength to ask them aloud.

Five hours later, with my wounds bandaged and consciousness regained, I sat in an interrogation room at the police station. It was 8 a.m., and the realization hit me that it was my daughter's birthday. I had missed so many of them. Years in prison had made me miss so much and, undoubtedly, now I would be heading back there. I laid my head flat on the metal conference room table, then gasped for breath. I was having an allergic reaction to the hydrocodone they had given me before I left the hospital. As my throat closed, I was dying for the second time that night.

3

HOMELESS

Years before the shooting, a guard called my name at the maximum-security penitentiary in Anamosa, Iowa, "Orth! Kyle Orth!" He was standing in front of my cell.

My sentence had been discharged.

Being released from prison was one of the most terrifying moments of my life.

The prison gates clanged shut behind me, marking the end of that chapter of my life, but I didn't feel free. It felt like I was stepping into an abyss. A sea of terrifying unknown. And cold. Freezing, life-threatening cold.

It was a bitterly cold Iowa winter, the kind where the air bites at any exposed skin and just drawing breath is a challenge. Snow covered everything, and the wind cut through my paper-thin prison-issued coat like I wasn't even wearing one. I was twenty-five years old, technically an adult, but in many ways still a child – inexperienced, scared, and utterly unprepared for the "real" world.

All I had to my name was one hundred dollars in cash, a pair of white prison sneakers, the summer-weight clothes I was wearing, and no idea what would come next. The prison guards dropped me off at the bus station in Cedar Rapids. I was the only one there. From that moment on, I was alone. No family to greet me, no friends to help me. I was homeless in the dead of winter, with nowhere to go and no one to turn to. My heart pounded. My thoughts swirled. I didn't arrive at the bus station like a free man, smiling and swinging a suitcase, joyful to be out of prison. I had been discarded there – dumped – left to navigate a world that I'd already proven that I was unable to navigate. It was as unforgiving as the concrete under my feet.

I stared at the peeling paint and worn posters that barely clung to the walls of the bus station. The night felt colder, heavier with grim possibilities. I swallowed hard, my inner voice screaming that I deserved better.

This wasn't the rebirth I'd envisioned. It was a treacherous path paved with harsh realities. I had dreamed of getting out of prison. That first night of "freedom" was a nightmare.

I tried to find somewhere – anywhere – to stay warm, but every corner of the city seemed to be as cold and frozen as I was.

That night I realized that if I laid down and went to sleep, I would freeze to death, so I walked the streets, kept moving to stay alive.

The next day, I alternated between the library and the bus station, napping there.

That became my routine for the next two weeks. Find warm places that would tolerate me being there for a couple of hours, constantly worried that they'd kick me out, napping the little bit that I could. Then at night, walk the streets to keep from freezing to death.

Hunger was my constant, relentless companion. It gnawed at me without a shred of mercy.

Without an ID or a Social Security card, getting into a shelter or accessing any kind of help was impossible. The bureaucratic loop was maddening: to get a Social Security card, they wanted to see my driver's license. You can't get a driver's license without a Social Security card. No ID, no help.

I was helpless.

One night, down in the dumpster behind KFC, I spotted it – a half-eaten piece of fried chicken with bits of wilted lettuce stuck to the skin. It was a grotesque mosaic of what had once been someone else's crispy meal. Every bit of it was repulsive.

I picked up the piece and inspected it under the glare of the lights in the parking lot. My stomach churned. I had never imagined my life would reach this low. In that moment, though, that chicken was all I had. The first bite was a jolt, a mix of salt and grease and the bitter taste of realizing that I was a complete failure. Each successive bite reminded me of the way the world had stripped away my dignity in exchange for a scrap of nourishment. Yet, with every swallow I had a fleeting hope that even in the depths of misery, I might find a way, someday, to reclaim a measure of my dignity.

The cold that winter was relentless.

It was not my first time being homeless, I learned how to be homeless at a young age.

This felt different. My fingers and toes ached constantly, and I began to worry about frostbite. The wind seemed to find every opening in my clothing, and it swirled and wrapped around me like an evil, life sucking embrace.

There were times when I thought I would not survive.

One night, as I curled up under a bridge with nothing but a lightweight blanket I'd found in the trash, I prayed for the first time in years. It wasn't a prayer of hope or faith, but of desperation: "God, if you're out there, don't let me die like this. Not like this!"

The cold does not wait for you under a bridge, it greets you before you get there. It hits in layers, like invisible hands stripping away whatever warmth you managed to hold on to. The concrete above your head sweats frost. Every sound is louder in the hollow space, every gust of wind takes on a life of its own. It slips through the gaps in the guardrail, slides down the pillars, curls around your ankles, then climbs your spine like it knows exactly where to find the spots that hurt the most.

Your breath hangs in the air in front of you, a little gray cloud that forms slow and disappears quick. If you sit still too long it feels like your lungs are inhaling metal shavings. The ground is frozen hard and uneven, the kind of hard that bruises you through your jeans before you realize you have started shaking. You try to layer cardboard, old flyers, maybe an abandoned pizza box, anything to build a thin barrier between you and the ice beneath you. It never works. Cold creeps through everything here. The cold here has the slow, steady, determined patience that the Midwest is known for. And it gets you.

Cars pass overhead with a rolling rumble, the kind you feel more than hear. Each one sends a soft vibration down through the concrete. Dust falls in little grains that cling to your clothes. Sometimes chunks of dirty snow tumble down from the edges when a truck goes by, landing close enough to spray you with cold specks. You brush them off, but they melt into the thin places in your gloves, and your fingertips sting.

Nights are the worst. The darkness under a bridge is not really dark, it is a dim blue mixed with the orange flicker of a streetlight half a block away. Shadows distort. You start to track sounds that do not matter. The crack of ice across the river. The distant bark of a dog. The sharp snap of your own teeth chattering. You tuck your chin against your chest and pull your coat tight, trapping whatever little body heat you can generate. You start rocking without meaning to. You do it because movement is the only thing standing between you and hypothermia.

Your hands hurt first. Then your ears. Then your feet. The cold climbs into your shoes through the thin rubber soles, numbing your toes until they feel like they belong to someone else. You curl them inside your socks, but it only helps for a second. Every once in a while you shake your feet hard to remind them they are still yours.

Sleep comes in shreds. Two minutes here. Five minutes there. You never fall all the way into it because the cold pushes you awake just as you start to drift. Your body jerks itself back alive, a survival instinct. You pull your arms in close to protect your ribs. You hold your breath for a second to feel your own heartbeat, to make sure it is still beating.

You start counting things in your head to distract yourself. The cars. The cracks in the concrete. The minutes until sunrise. You imagine what warm feels like. Not summer, not heat, just warm enough to stop shaking. Warm enough to feel your fingers bend without pain.

Sometimes a gust of wind hits wrong and you lose the air in your chest. It feels like someone reached through your jacket and crushed your lungs. You cough because it is the only response your body can offer. The sound echoes under the bridge, bouncing back at you until it feels like there are two of you sitting there, both barely hanging on.

The smell of river water drifts through every now and then. Cold river water has a scent that is sharp and earthy, almost metallic. It reminds you that there are places colder than this frigid spot under the bridge, and it comes as no consolation.

By morning the cardboard beneath you has softened, sagged, maybe even frozen to the shape of your body. Standing up is slow. Your muscles fight you. Your joints crack. Your feet feel like they are wrapped in glass. You rub your hands together until they burn because the burn means you made it through another night.

You walk out from under the bridge and the sunlight hurts at first. Your eyes water. The wind feels harsher in the open, but something in you still loosens a little the moment you step out. You survived the dark. You survived the cold that lives inside that concrete cave.

And in your pocket or deep in your chest, you carry the smallest ember of hope, the tiny fire that stays smoldering even when everything around you is frozen.

4

BLUE GRASS

My life was not always this way.

The earliest memories I have are a blur of constant tension, turbulence, and fear. Of screaming, slammed doors, broken bottles, and upended chairs. Of threats and arguments, of my cowering with my siblings from raging grown-ups.

I was the youngest of seven, the baby in a broken family. My mother was a force of nature, wild and unpredictable. Her mood changed without warning. Her expressions of love were as fleeting as her moments of sobriety. My father was a ghost in my life, gone before I could remember. Though I had six brothers and sisters, I often felt alone.

When I was around three years old, my mother married Jeff. He was a decent man in many ways…a bit of an eccentric, he was obsessed with high-performance Italian motorcycles. He preferred the hum of an engine to the noise of children. He didn't dislike me, but he didn't particularly know what to do with me either, so he mostly just let me be. That was a gift in a house that often felt like a battlefield. Without Jeff, we would have been drowning in poverty.

We lived on an acreage outside of Blue Grass, Iowa, on a stretch of land surrounded by thick beautiful woods. While the house was filled with yelling, broken dishes, and the unpredictable wrath of my mother, the outside was different. The woods became my sanctuary. The trees didn't scream at me, and the wind didn't slap me across the face. The woods were my escape, a place where my imagination could run wild, where I could be anything other than a scared little boy in a chaotic home.

She came at me with a butcher knife once.

I was seven. Maybe eight. Just a little kid.

Her eyes were glassy, far off, like she wasn't looking at me at all, like she was staring through me at something no one else could see. The screaming had started hours earlier. I don't remember what triggered it. I never did. That was the worst part. You never knew what would set her off.

One minute she was Mom. The next, she was a storm.

I ran – barefoot, heart thudding in my chest – and didn't stop until the chaos of our house was hidden by the trees behind it.

If you've ever run through the trees with your heart pounding from something other than joy, you might understand.

Her words were like razor blades, her hands as unpredictable as the Midwestern weather in spring. I was too young to name what was happening, too small to stop it, and too afraid to speak of it.

But I had one sacred place:

The woods.

The woods began just behind our property, past the rusted swing set and the chain-link fence that sagged like it had given up hope.

The woods became my sanctuary. My cathedral. My favorite place.

There was something holy to me in that tangle of branches and bark. The wind was a hymn through the leaves, and the sun danced like stained glass on the forest floor. I didn't have a Bible back then. I didn't even know what salvation meant, but I felt Him. Deep in my bones, like a whisper I didn't yet have words for.

"He who dwells in the secret place of the Most High shall abide under the shadow of the Almighty." - Psalm 91:1

That was it. I didn't know that verse as a kid, but I knew that feeling. In the shadow of those towering oaks and whispering maples, I was hidden. Covered. Protected.

God.

I didn't see Him, but I felt Him. I'd close my eyes and talk to the wind, somehow knowing it carried my voice to heaven. I didn't pray like grown-ups do. I prayed the way only a child who's desperate and untouched by religion can pray; raw, from the gut, sometimes with words. And He answered. Not with words. With presence.

The woods were God's mercy to me. A safe haven He carved out just for one frightened boy in a broken home.

Some kids find God in church pews. I found Him in pine needles and deer trails.

It was like the Lord Himself walked those woods, waiting for me.

I don't think it's a coincidence that Jesus often withdrew to quiet places to pray. Luke 5:16 says, "But Jesus often withdrew to lonely places and prayed." He knew what I didn't: that silence is sacred. That stillness can be holy. That even in chaos, you can find peace when you run to the Father.

I didn't know that yet, but the woods taught me.

They taught me how to dream. How to believe. How to survive.

I was a sweet little boy. I felt emotions deeply and sensed the feelings of others. When others hurt, I sympathized and tried to tenderly console them. When an animal was hurt, I pitied it and tried to comfort it. Of all the things that shaped me, it was that early tenderness – my sweetness and kindness – that made everything hurt so much worse. I wasn't built for the kind of violence I saw in my home. I wasn't born with an intrinsic defense system.

Are any of us?

I came into the world with my heart wide open, and for a long time I kept believing that if I loved hard enough, if I was good enough, if I *tried* hard enough, maybe the storm in my mother would calm down. Maybe my home could be safe. Maybe she could see me the way I saw her – flawed, sure, but someday we'd be okay. I believed I could convince my mom to love me. I clung to the hope that someday I could be enough for her, even though all her actions told me there was no hope for that.

Most nights, I'd lie awake long after the shouting had died down, trying to piece together what I had done wrong. Was it the way I talked? The way I walked? Had I smiled at the wrong moment? Or not smiled enough? I blamed myself for my mother's cruelty. I believed that it must be all my fault. It was easier than accepting the truth; that her brokenness was deeper and older than anything I could understand.

Our household was governed by invisible rules that shifted like the wind across the corn fields. Some days I could make my mother laugh, and for a few golden minutes, I was just a boy and she was just my mom, and it almost felt normal. I lived for those moments, held onto them and savored them, but they never lasted. They couldn't, because eventually the bottle would be empty, her anger would rise, and the cycle would begin again, faster than I could scramble out of her way.

Outside, the world kept turning. School, neighbors, the woods – those were places where other kids enjoyed simpler lives. I envied those kids without even understanding what I was envying. I carried a sadness inside me, a heavy, aching thing that made me feel older than the other boys my age. I laughed when they laughed, I ran when they ran, but something in me was always watching, always waiting for the ground to shift under my feet like it did at home.

If you'd met me back then, you might have thought I was just shy, or maybe a little too eager to please. You wouldn't have seen the scars hidden under the sleeves of my hand-me-down shirts, or the bruises I learned to explain away with stories about clumsy falls and accidents. You wouldn't have known that I could gauge the mood of a room with a single glance, or sense the tension that simmered under the surface of a relationship but wasn't acknowledged outwardly. Kindness was still my instinct, but trust became a thing I rationed carefully, almost unknowingly, like a resource too precious to waste on just anyone.

Survival in an abusive home teaches you skills like that, skills no child should have to master.

For all the damage, for all the ways my years in that house toughened me up, they didn't kill the part of me that wanted to love and be loved. They battered it and bruised it, but somehow it survived, tucked deep inside, waiting for a day when it wouldn't have to be a bargaining chip. It lay dormant, waiting for something real, something lasting, something that didn't hurt.

The worst pain wasn't physical, it was the pain of rejection I felt in my heart. My fear of my mother never faded; it only settled deeper, a particular pain that made a home in my bones. I learned to move quietly, to make myself small, to anticipate the storm before it hit. I told myself it was normal, that I just had to endure it. But something inside me cracked a little more each time. I didn't know how to process the anger, the shame, and the feeling that I was nothing more than a punching bag for my mother's frustration. So I buried it. I shoved it down deep, where even I couldn't reach it. It would fester there for years, poisoning the way I saw myself and the way I trusted others.

My sisters Tracy and Toni had it worse than I did, maybe because they had a different dad, or maybe because they were older. Or maybe because they were young and beautiful, and my mom knew her own beauty was fleeting. She had been pretty once, too, but the drinking, the rage, and years of bitterness had stolen that from her. She saw her daughters growing into the kind of women she could never be, and instead of loving them for it, she hated them, resented them, and made sure they suffered for it.

Bruises and black eyes were a regular thing for them. The school staff noticed it on them before they ever noticed it on me, maybe because they were girls or maybe because they had it significantly rougher. Teachers would pull them aside, whispering questions and acting concerned, but nothing ever changed. Nothing ever stopped the beatings. The bruises would fade, but we all knew they'd be replaced with fresh ones before long. It was a cycle that never ended.

The worst night came when Mom nearly killed Tracy. Mom was in one of her blackouts, those terrifying states when she became something else entirely, something savage with no limits and no mercy. I don't remember what set her off; it could've been anything. Tracy might have rolled her eyes. Maybe she sighed too loudly. Or maybe she just existed in the wrong place at the wrong time. It didn't matter. One second Mom was screaming and the next, she had Tracy by the throat and was shoving her against the wall so hard the whole house seemed to shake.

Tracy's feet barely touched the ground. Her face turned red, then purple. She clawed at Mom's hands, trying to break free. But when Mom was drunk, she was an electrified wire, thin but strong and pulsing with lethal power. And this time, she was ugly with jealousy, emptied of her humanity, any sense of maternal instinct – she was blind uncaged rage.

For a moment, I thought this was it. I thought I was about to watch my sister die.

Our sister Toni screamed. I stood there, frozen, my heart pounding, my mind blank. Then, miraculously, for once, Jeff stepped in. He pried Mom off Tracy, yanking her away before she could finish what she started. She turned on him, wild-eyed and furious, swinging, cursing, the rage pouring toward him. But Jeff could take it. And he wasn't the one she wanted to destroy anyway.

Tracy collapsed to the floor, gasping for air, her throat bruised, her body trembling. She didn't cry. She never did. No matter how bad it got, she held it in, as if she was refusing to give Mom the satisfaction. The police came and, because the system is flawed and often sides with the woman in domestic situations, Jeff ended up in jail for a few nights. It didn't matter that he was just trying to restrain Mom and keep her from killing Tracy. The law saw what it wanted to see, and Jeff paid the price for his attempts at intervention. I wanted to hate Jeff for his weakness and his inability to protect Tracy and all of us. But deep down, I knew he was just as trapped as we were. He wasn't a bad man. He was just a man who had made the mistake of loving and marrying my mother.

The next morning, Tracy went to school with the bruises still fresh around her neck, dark like a noose. Nobody said a word. Nobody ever did. We all learned that where we lived, speaking up never made a difference.

But then, one day, it did.

Someone noticed.

Cared.

Our school principal, Mrs. White, took Tracy and Toni in. I felt relief for them, but also a deep, aching loneliness. They were safe now but I wasn't. I was left in the house with Jeff and my mother, trapped between his quiet indifference and her relentless fury. I had no buffer now, no shield between Mom's fury and me. And I knew it was only a matter of time before she turned it all on me.

My brother Justin had gotten out before I could even remember. He was the oldest, and in a way, he was the luckiest. He got to escape and live with our grandparents in Florida, far away from Mom's drunken rages and the constant fear that came with them. I was jealous of him for that. He got the life I wanted; a life without bruises, without screaming, without walking on eggshells every second of the day. But I also knew he hadn't left unscathed. He had gotten his share before he was sent away. Mom had beaten him down, too, until someone finally stepped in.

Still, it never felt fair. While Tracy, Toni, and I were stuck living in hell, Justin was playing on beaches, going to Disney World, living a life that might as well have been on another planet. Every once in a while, he'd send me things: Mickey Mouse stuffed animals or Tampa Bay Buccaneers gear. I liked the gifts, or I wanted to like them. But at the same time, I resented them. They were reminders of the life he had and the one I didn't have. I'd hold the stuffed animals and wonder if he had even thought about what it was like for me, if he remembered what it felt like to be afraid all the time, if he ever felt guilty that he got out and we didn't.

So Justin and I were never close. How could we be? He was a faint memory, someone who existed in the background of my life, technically a brother but practically – at best – a pen pal. I don't know if it was because of the distance or because we had such different lives, but there was always a wall between us.

He never really understood what it was like for me growing up in that house after he left, just like I could never understand what it was like for him before he went. Maybe that's why I never knew what to say to him. I wanted to hate him for getting out, but deep down, I knew it wasn't his fault. He had suffered, too. He had just been lucky enough to escape.

School was another battleground for me. Sitting still was nearly impossible. My body buzzed with restless energy, and the structure of a classroom felt suffocating. I got into trouble constantly, not because I was bad, but because I couldn't force myself to conform to the expectations of a quiet, obedient student. I was different. My mind was somewhere else, often lost in the woods around my house, where I could be anything, where I was free.

They gave me a place to be a child, to dream, to escape. And in those moments when I was surrounded by nothing but trees and the endless sky, I could almost believe I was free. But unfortunately, no matter how much I escaped into my imagination, reality always came rushing back. No matter how deep I went into the woods, I always had to come home.

Looking back, I don't know how I survived those years.

But the truth is, something in me also started to break. The anger, the fear, the helplessness all began to twist inside me, changing me in ways I couldn't understand as a little boy. Slowly, I started to change. I stopped feeling as deeply, stopped caring as much.

I started becoming mean.

The change did not happen in one moment. It crept in like cold air through a cracked window.

At first, there was still that soft part of me, the kid who used to line up toy cars, admiring their colors. The kid who hugged the dog too tight because love felt bigger than his little body could hold. That part of me was still there. But the house had its own weather, and it was always storm season. I learned early that footsteps could predict the sky. Slow ones meant I could breathe. Fast ones meant I should disappear.

Her voice carried the scorch of liquor before you could smell it on her breath.

I learned to see it in her jaw, how it tightened. I learned the warning sign of her eyes narrowing. Every time she whipped around on me, something in me flinched. Got smaller. And another part of me hardened.

I would sit at the table, fingers tracing the grooves in the wood, listening to the bottle clink against the counter. I used to pray she would stay in a good mood. Later, I stopped praying for that. I just prayed her aim would be off.

There were nights when she grabbed my shirt and shook me, her words slurred, her breath hot with whiskey. Tears used to come easy then. Later, they stopped showing up. My face learned not to move. My voice learned not to tremble.

Like Toni's had.

I started snapping at people for no reason. Teachers. Kids. Anyone who looked at me too long. It felt good for a second, like releasing steam from a boiling pot. I didn't know then that I was practicing the language of survival. I only knew that being sweet made me a target in my own home, and I was done being an easy target.

The first time I shoved a kid on the playground, it surprised me how steady my hands were. No shaking. No guilt. Just a quick jolt of power, sharp and clean, and for a moment I felt bigger than the thing that scared me at home.

Later, I realized I didn't feel bad at all when I hurt someone.

That scared me more than anything she ever did.

I can look back as an adult and see that boy, see little me, little Kyle.

I could write him a letter:

> *"You stopped looking people in the eyes when you talked. Your shoulders rounded, ready to take a hit. Your jaw stayed tight, ready to bite back. And somewhere in the mix of slammed doors, broken promises, and slurred threats, the sweet kid started fading into the background like an old photograph left in the sun."*
>
> *"Nobody noticed the exact day he disappeared. The sweet little boy. But you did. You noticed it every time you opened your mouth and heard her voice instead of your own."*

And then one terrible day when I was about eight years old, my mom and Jeff said they had some news. They told me we were moving to Davenport. There would be no more woods ... no more escape.

5

STEPPING OFF THE EDGE OF THE WORLD

Moving the fifteen miles to Davenport felt like stepping off the edge of the world. The wide wild woods of Blue Grass, the only sanctuary I'd ever known, were traded for a grid of congested streets, cracked sidewalks, sagging porches, and endless noise. The trees that once towered over me like ancient guardians were replaced by telephone poles and streetlights. The air even felt different, tinged with exhaust and a sense of unfamiliarity. In Blue Grass, even when home was a battle-field, I could always run into the trees and let them swallow me up. In Davenport there was nowhere to run, nowhere to disappear. Just miles of houses with strangers' windows staring back at me.

I hated it immediately and completely. Everything about the city rubbed me the wrong way. The endless rows of houses made me feel trapped, like the walls were closing in on me.

Out in the country the world used to feel open, like it stretched out forever in all directions. I could step off the porch and the world invited me. The wind carried the smells of dirt and hay. The sounds of country, of bugs and wind in the grass and tractors and birds were the soundtrack to a happy life. I could disappear into the treeline anytime I wanted. One step and I was swallowed in thick green peace. Branches brushed my arms like familiar hands. The woods were a hiding place and a breathing place and a thinking place. In there I could hear my own heartbeat without anybody trying to drown it out.

The first morning I woke up in Davenport, it was inside the confines of claustrophobic walls. The air tasted like metal. The houses sat shoulder to shoulder like they were arguing. Every sound stacked on top of the next, the buzz of cars, the bark of a dog, the slam of some stranger's door. These sounds didn't blend into the romantic harmony of a bustling city; each noise cut the others, and me. I kept looking for grass that was wild and natural, not trimmed into squares, confined inside concrete corners. I kept trying to find a dirt trail that led away from everything. But the only paths were sidewalks that forced you to stay in the open where everyone could see you.

In the country, you could run and nobody asked where you were going. In the city, there were eyes everywhere and it felt like they were all watching me. My shoulders pulled up on their own. My steps got shorter. The sky seemed smaller. I would scan the alley to see if there was a way out, but there never was. Just more brick, more windows, more eyes watching me. I kept trying to breathe the way I used to breathe back home but my chest stayed tight like I had a belt snugged up under my armpits, around my ribcage.

Some nights I would close my eyes and picture the woods. I would remember the smell of damp leaves and that narrow trail that cut down the hill. But the city sounds forced their way in through the window: sirens, voices, engines – they drove away the memory. The place that used to give me peace was gone, and this new place was a thief of peace.

Out there I was free. In here I was cornered.

I was a kid carrying too much baggage, and Davenport just piled more weight onto my back.

Starting at a new school was like trying to breathe under water. Every hallway echoed with laughter that wasn't meant for me and conversations I didn't know how to join. I was angry and out of place, full of grief and rage, despite being too young to name those emotions. The first morning at the new school felt like stepping into a room where everyone already knew the plan except me. My stomach twisted tight while I stood in the hallway, pretending to study the cracks in the tile so I did not have to meet anyone's eyes. The air smelled like bleach and cafeteria food, and I felt totally alone.

Back home, slammed cupboards and slurred voices signaled the coming storm inside the house. When the atmosphere shifted, it rarely shifted for the better. So walking into this building with its buzzing lights and crowded noise felt like bracing for something to go wrong. My shoulders were already pulled up like I was expecting a hit, even though no one here even knew my name yet.

Kids brushed past me in clusters. Backpacks bumped me. Lockers clanged open. Somewhere down the hall someone laughed loudly, unrestrained, and it felt like they were laughing at me. The woods were gone. The place where you could disappear without asking permission … gone. Out there, branches moved with the wind; not with moods. Nothing in those trees ever shifted suddenly just to scare me.

Here everything felt hard and bright and unpredictable. Teachers' voices echoed from doorways with instructions I could not remember. My hands shook a little when I reached for the pencil on my desk, like my body was waiting for something to explode even though the room stayed calm.

The bell rang and everyone moved like they knew exactly where to go. I hesitated because the sound felt too familiar, sharp and sudden, the kind of sound that used to mean trouble was coming. My legs knew how to run, but they did not know how to walk confidently down this hallway. So I followed the crowd and kept my head low. My chest stayed tight all day, tighter every time someone looked at me too long or asked me a simple question I could not answer correctly.

By the time the final bell rang, releasing me from this first day at a new school, I walked out of the building feeling hollow. I was a kid who had been dropped into someone else's life. I had to go back to a house where there were no trees waiting for me. No quiet hiding place. No familiar footsteps of a best friend walking beside me. Only a long stretch of sidewalk and the dull ache of knowing there was no going back.

But then there was Miss Brown.

Miss Brown was a beacon of light in a world of darkness, and even at my young age, I knew she was different. She wasn't just another adult going through the motions. Miss Brown had a way of standing beside me that made the harsh, abrasive classroom feel bearable. She never hovered. She never sighed the long, tired sigh that said I was too much for her. She just settled in like someone who had all the time in the world, even though I knew she didn't. Other adults talked over kids, talked around them, talked like they were delivering orders. Miss Brown listened. Not the stiff kind of listening when a grownup folds their arms and waits for you to stop talking. Her eyes softened a little. Her shoulders relaxed. It was the kind of listening that made me realize she was picking up more than my words. She was catching the parts I tried to hide.

She noticed things. Small things. The way my leg bounced under the desk when my stomach carried too much fear. The way I scanned the room before answering a question, because home had trained me to see danger before speaking. She never pointed it out. She never corrected me in front of the class. She just shifted the whole atmosphere so I didn't feel like I had to brace for something.

Most adults kept their distance from me, like they were afraid trouble might rub off on them. Miss Brown pulled chairs up closer, not because she needed to say anything urgent but because she wanted me to know I was worth sitting beside. She handed back papers without that look other teachers gave, that tight little expression that said I was a problem they were required to solve. With her, my name came out warm. Like she saw the kid I was before life twisted me up.

When she laughed, it wasn't the polite kind that teachers use. It was a real laugh that cracked open the room. For a second it felt like I was not the kid from the chaotic house or the kid who was mentally checked out half the time. I was just a kid with her. A regular kid. And she treated me like I belonged there. Like belonging was not something I had to earn by being perfect. It was mine just for showing up.

She never acted shocked by anything I did or didn't do. She never leaned away the way some adults did when they realized my life did not match theirs. There was no pity in her face. No fear. No frustration. She stayed steady. In a world where adults blew hot and cold, she was… even. Predictable. Safe in a way I didn't have language for yet.

It was subtle. But I felt it. Every time she knelt to my eye level instead of looking down on me. Every time she gave me a second to gather my thoughts instead of rushing me on. Every time she remembered some tiny detail I had casually mentioned days before. She carried my story gently. That was the difference. Other adults wanted to fix me or avoid me. Miss Brown just saw me.

And being seen that way, even for a few minutes in a classroom lit under cold fluorescent lights, it felt like finding a warm, safe place in a world that never stopped shaking.

She moved through our third-grade classroom with authority. Her voice, when it rose, had a rhythm that commanded respect without crushing our spirits. She wore bright, beautiful clothes – yellows, reds, blues – that made her stand out in a sea of gray and beige, just like her spirit did. She carried herself like she knew exactly who she was, and like she had no interest in apologizing for it. For a kid like me, who had grown up watching adults either explode in anger or shrink into their addictions, she was something altogether new: strong, steady, and kind.

Most importantly, Miss Brown *saw* me, really saw me. Not just the problems I caused or the restless energy I couldn't control, but the bruised and hurting boy underneath it all. Where others saw me as a disruption, she saw potential. Where others saw a future dropout, she somehow caught a glimpse of the boy I might become if someone – anyone – believed in me. And when she looked at me, I started to wonder if she might be right. Maybe I wasn't just the sum of my scars and screw-ups. Maybe there was more to me than I'd been told.

In a year when everything else in my world felt like it was falling apart, Miss Brown quietly helped me hold things together inside myself. They were things I wouldn't fully understand for many years to come, but they were real and necessary all the same: the belief that I was worth seeing, worth investing in, worth loving. And for a kid like me, that was everything.

Miss Brown even helped me find my dad.

It felt like we were chasing a ghost. All I had was a last name—"Orth"—and a faint memory that he had once worked at Quaker Oats, a cereal manufacturer in Cedar Rapids, Iowa, eighty-five miles to the west. That was it. My mom kept that part of my life story tightly sealed, like a door bolted shut and, in this case, hidden behind layers of bitterness. Every time I asked about my dad, it was like I'd lit a match in a room full of gas fumes. Her anger would explode, wild and disproportionate to the size of my inquiry. I learned to keep my questions to myself. Still, deep inside, I clung to a stubborn belief that my dad had loved me once, or at least wanted to love me. I told myself a story that made it easier to bear: that he hadn't stayed because fighting my mother would've been like swimming against a riptide, and he just didn't have the strength. Probably nobody would.

But Miss Brown didn't believe in leaving any stones unturned. She thought kids deserved answers to their questions, even the hardest ones. So she helped me. She made a few calls, pieced together bits of information she found, and somehow, against the odds, she found him.

My first meeting with my dad was a jarring collision of my idealistic expectations and … reality. I don't know what I had imagined. Maybe a tall, smiling figure waiting with open arms? A Hallmark movie moment where everything wrong in my life would somehow be righted? He wasn't that. He was just a man. A man with tired eyes, a work-worn face, and a life that didn't include me. He had other kids, kids who bore his last name proudly and called him "Dad" without hesitation. Kids who knew his laugh, who had grown up with his presence like the furniture in a familiar house. I had none of those things. I was an afterthought, a chapter in his life story that he hadn't intended to reopen.

Each visit to my dad's house with his "new" family was a reminder that I didn't belong there. Their smiles toward me were polite but a little suspicious. I was a stranger at a family reunion, and I didn't know the players, the history, or the inside jokes. I stood at the edge of their easy conversations, aching to find an invisible door I could walk through and somehow belong. But there wasn't such a door, and there never would be.

Still, for a while, I pretended. I told myself that just being near him was enough, that at least I wasn't completely forgotten. But inside, the ache gnawed deeper, confirming a truth that I was too young to put into words: Sometimes, the people you long for the most are the ones who can't love you back. No matter how much you want it, no matter how much you try to squeeze yourself into their world, you're left standing outside, looking in.

When the pain of that rejection got too intense, it was Miss Brown's voice that steadied me. She didn't try to patch the hole in my heart with pretty lies. Instead, she gave me something stronger: hope. Hope did not arrive in a speech or a lesson. It came in little pieces, almost too small to notice at first. Miss Brown would slide them your way without making a scene, the same way someone might hand you a coat without calling attention to the cold.

It was the way she looked at me when I walked into the room. Other adults scanned me like they were checking for the day's damage. She looked at me like she expected me to make it. Like she saw a future ahead of me even when I didn't see anything but fog.

She caught me on the days I came in raw from the night before. Not by pulling me aside, not by asking questions I wasn't ready to answer. She just steadied the day around me. She slowed down the day. Softened it. Created the kind of place where my breath could finally catch up.

When she handed back my work, she tapped her finger next to the one thing I did right instead of circling the seven things I did wrong. That tiny gesture felt like someone cracking open a window in a room I thought I would suffocate in. It told me maybe I wasn't broken in every way. Maybe I had something left in me worth nurturing.

On the days I shut down, she didn't write me off. She didn't toss my name into the same pile everyone else did. She crouched beside my desk, not to correct me, but to anchor me. She spoke in a calm voice that soaked through the panic. It told me, without saying it, that I was not alone inside my own head.

She remembered things about me that most adults forgot as soon as I walked away. A detail. A joke. Something small I liked. Hope showed up in those moments like a spark catching wet wood. Surprising, faint at first, but with the potential to dry the wood and catch fire. She treated me like the story was not written yet. Like the chapters ahead weren't certain, weren't already determined by the chaos I came from. Like this could be a comeback story, and not a sad predictable tragedy.

Under her care, I learned that love wasn't always about DNA or shared last names. Sometimes love could come from other people in our lives, could come through small yet significant acts of kindness.

But then, just like that, third grade ended and that little classroom, the only safe place in my life, closed to me. Once again, I was left standing at the edge … hoping, bracing, wondering if anything good could really last.

6

BEHAVIORAL DISORDERS

Fourth grade was another storm without a shelter. Without Miss Brown to anchor me and create some cover, I began to unravel. I lost what little focus I had. I stopped caring about school at all. I started getting into more trouble, not because I was mean-spirited, but because without her believing in me, it felt like no one did or ever would. Nobody else saw me the way she had, like I was worth saving. Nobody else bothered to see the hurting boy underneath the chaotic behavior.

When they placed me in behavioral disorder classes (BD), it was a relief.

It felt like the system was finally admitting what everyone – including me and my mom – had always suspected: that I was a lost cause. I can still remember the smell of the smaller classrooms and the sense of resignation that filled the air. We weren't students who were at school to learn; we were being managed. The goal wasn't education, it was containment. They wanted to keep us distracted enough to avoid a meltdown, so they rewarded good behavior not with learning but with video games and candy. It was like being warehoused. There seemed to be a quiet agreement that we were not going to improve. Nobody expected us to.

At first, the incentives felt great. We had a pizza party if a week passed without an incident. What kid doesn't love a pizza party?

We got extra recess time for not throwing a chair. It was absurd, but at nine years old, what did I know? It didn't take long to figure out that bad behavior was a kind of currency, an odd dance where acting out brought more attention, more negotiation, and eventually even more rewards. And even though I started out as just a hyperactive kid desperate for connection, it was impossible not to get pulled into the gravitational force of the older kids who had already given up on playing by the rules. Survival in that world didn't mean learning how to be better. It meant learning how to blend in and mask whatever soft, caring, vulnerable pieces of me still remained.

As the months dragged on, I stopped seeing myself as anything but what they told me I was: a troublemaker, a lost cause, and a boy who couldn't be trusted. I watched how the older boys talked, how they moved, how they wore their defiance like knights wore armor, and I imitated it without even realizing I was doing it. It wasn't that I wanted to be that way, it was that the environment made it clear that this was how I was going to succeed in a world that didn't expect anything good from me. I stopped expecting it from myself, too.

Looking back, I can see it now for what it was: a slow erasure.

It didn't erase who I was at my core, but it wiped away who I thought I could become.

BD classes didn't teach me how to get better; they taught me how to give up.

It planted seeds in my soil that said, "I am a mistake, a failure."

That plant grew roots that would take years, and a lot of pain, to eventually rip out.

As I got older, I realized that the system had failed me. The BD classes were a short-term solution but they were creating a long-term problem. They kept us out of trouble for the moment but did nothing to address the deeper issues we were all facing. It wasn't until much later that I began to see how much I had internalized that "bad kid" persona and how difficult it would be to break out of it. The classes were meant to contain us, but in many ways, they also capped our potential. I had let my environment shape who I was, not realizing how difficult it would be to unlearn that identity as I grew up.

By sixth grade, it wasn't just that I had started slipping into the cracks, it was like I had been swallowed by them. Home had long since stopped feeling like home, and school held no hope for me. I was too young to even grasp what "dropping out" really meant; all I knew was that I couldn't I wouldn't – keep showing up to a place that made me feel smaller with every passing day. So one day, I just didn't go. One day turned into two, then a week, then a month. Before anyone bothered to ask where I was, I was already gone. I turned my back on school and my "home."

The streets of Davenport, with their cold concrete and harsh streetlights, became my world. It was a strange place to live, but I learned how to quickly. At least out here, the rules were clear: survive, or don't. I became a ghost floating among people with normal lives; an invisible, wiry figure slipping through alleys, scaling fences, always on the lookout for opportunity. I slept where I could: threadbare couches in strangers' homes when luck was on my side, the floorboards of unlocked cars or the crawl spaces under porches when it wasn't. I was constantly hungry, sometimes to the point that my body trembled and my thinking got fuzzy. There were nights when the cold penetrated so deep into my bones that I thought maybe I'd just freeze where I lay, and a small, exhausted part of this middle-school aged boy welcomed the idea.

But something stubborn in me always fought to survive. Some spark of my fire to live refused to go out, no matter how lonely or miserable I felt. I told myself this life was better than what I'd left behind in Blue Grass, and maybe in some ways, it was.

At least the pain out here made sense.

It didn't come from my mother, who was supposed to be safe and loving, but who wasn't.

7

RUNAWAY

I didn't set out to be a thief.

It started with survival – just a middle-school aged kid looking for something to fill my stomach and a warm place to crash. But survival has a way of blurring the lines between need and want. What began as sneaking into empty garages and grabbing scraps soon morphed into something more deliberate. I learned to read neighborhoods like a map, memorizing which driveways stayed unoccupied the longest, or which windows were left cracked open on cool evenings. It wasn't hard for me to make myself invisible; adults barely saw their own kids, let alone a street rat like me.

Sometimes I'd knock on a door, just to be sure no one was home. If someone answered, I'd mumble a halfhearted lie about a lost dog, and they'd dismiss me with a tight smile or an annoyed wave. They didn't see me as a threat, just a nuisance. I took advantage of that.

When the coast was clear, I'd slip around the back and test the doors, windows, anything that might give. Once inside a house, it was like the world outside ceased to exist. For a moment, I could steal a piece of this life that was otherwise inaccessible to me. I couldn't hope to ever achieve this status, but for a few moments, it was mine.

I never lingered longer than I had to. I'd snatch a few granola bars from the pantry. A sweatshirt that had been tossed over a chair. Sometimes, if I felt desperate enough, I'd pocket loose change or any item I could trade for a hot meal. I didn't think about the families I was robbing or the fear they might feel upon discovering their homes had been violated. To me, they were faceless and nameless.

I didn't think about how it would feel for someone to walk into their home and see that things were gone. The idea that I was taking something precious from someone else didn't even occur to me. All I saw were houses waiting for someone like me to come along and take what I needed. I wasn't a thief; I was just a kid doing what I had to in order to keep body and soul together. I had learned early on that if I thought too much about the people in the houses, guilt would consume me. And I couldn't afford to feel guilty. I was too busy fighting to stay alive.

As time went on, it changed.

Anything that felt like guilt faded away.

I stopped fearing getting caught and started to be seduced by the thrill.

Breaking into places became a game of nerves. How fast could I get in and out, how invisible could I make myself?

Every successful run made me bolder and a little cockier. I convinced myself I was smart, untouchable even, when in truth, I was just a scared, broken kid gambling with his future because he didn't believe he had one.

Looking back now, it's almost unbearable to imagine a child living like that: Hungry, homeless, feral in a city that had no home for him. But at the time, it didn't feel like tragedy. It felt normal. It was my normal. And when you're barely surviving, you don't spend much time mourning the life you should have had. You just keep moving and taking whatever you can.

I didn't think about the consequences. I just did what I had to do, breaking into one house at a time. And when I was done, my thoughts were focused solely on the next step, without a care for the damage I was leaving behind.

Growing up, my best friend on the streets was a kid named Bobby. Bobby had a knack for finding me no matter where I ended up. It didn't matter if I crashed in some stranger's abandoned garage or tucked myself away behind the bleachers at an empty ball field, somehow Bobby always showed up. He was in the foster system, and he hated it with a passion. He made no effort to hide how much he hated his foster families. Every time he ran, it wasn't just from a house; it was from the feeling that he didn't belong anywhere. And every time he ran, he came looking for the one person who understood – me.

Bobby was my age and wiry like me, but with a face that looked a little too serious for a kid. Although his eyes were sad, his smile – when you could coax it out of him – lit up the room and hinted that he was still holding on to a thread of hope. He wasn't tough the way a lot of street kids pretended to be. He didn't put up the walls or the mean mug. Instead, he was open in a way that made him both brave and vulnerable, and it made me fiercely protective of him, even when I didn't know how to protect myself.

We had more adventures than I can count, like sneaking into construction sites after dark, pretending we were building kingdoms of our own. Or scavenging through alleys and back lots, looking for anything we could turn into food or cash. Some nights we stayed up for hours, perched on rooftops, making up stories about the lights in the distance. We wondered who lived in those houses, what their lives were like.

Bobby never talked much about the homes he left behind, nor the bruises, the long nights lying awake, listening for footsteps outside his door. But you didn't have to ask. It was apparent in the way he flinched at sudden noises, in the way he always kept one eye on the nearest exit. The streets were dangerous, sure. But to Bobby, they were still better than being trapped somewhere he wasn't wanted, pretending he was okay. Out here, with all its chaos and risk, at least there was a kind of freedom. Out here, he could breathe.

Even now, I sometimes wonder what would have happened if someone had caught him in time. What if an adult could have seen past the running and the anger and the walls he tried to build? A grownup who understood that Bobby was just a kid desperate for love. But back then, we didn't have anyone like that. We had each other. And as kids, we thought it was enough.

It wasn't.

Bobby had always been more cautious, more thoughtful, than I was. It was like some part of him still believed there were rules we were supposed to follow. Me? That part of me was dead. I lived for the pulse, for the way the night stretched out in front of us like a road only we could see. When we spotted the house, a sprawling, manicured monster tucked away past the tree line, it wasn't even a question for me. It was opportunity. It was oxygen that would save me from suffocation.

As we approached the house, Bobby hung back, shifting from foot to foot, his hands stuffed deep into the pockets of his hoodie.

"I don't know, man," he muttered, chewing the inside of his lip. "That place looks...different. That's a big house."

"Exactly," I said, my grin stretching wider. "Means better stuff inside."

Even as I spoke, I felt the familiar heat rise up in me, that feverish certainty that this night could change everything. Bobby was staring at the second-story deck. It was a wall he knew he couldn't climb. I was already calculating angles, distances, using my mind to feel the give of the wood under my hands.

When you lived like we did, you learned to see the world for where it was vulnerable. Where it could be exploited.

The climb was nothing. A quick scramble up the wood lattice and a leap of faith over the deck railing. My fingers brushed against splintery wood and iron railings slick with dew, but I didn't falter. I could hear Bobby's breath hitching from below as I reached the sliding glass door. Locked, of course. But locks were just suggestions. With a practiced lift and a soft pop, the sliding door gave way.

Once inside, I could sense that the people who lived here trusted the world too much. They believed a nice neighborhood and a tall fence could keep the darkness out. I slipped through the silence like the house belonged to me, the plush carpet absorbing the sound of my steps.

I stepped back outside onto the deck, and I waved Bobby up. He hesitated – he always hesitated – but his loyalty to me was stronger than his fear of getting caught. It always had been that way with him. He clambered up awkwardly, and I pulled him inside before he could lose his nerve.

"Stick close," I whispered.

We moved down the wide hallways, past framed family portraits and fancy furniture. We didn't belong in houses like this, but that never stopped us.

We were shadows.

We were hungry.

And we were quick.

The master bedroom was like an oversized treasure chest full of gems.

Quickly, we were pirates prying open the treasure chest.

I spotted a glass case full of rifles lined up like museum pieces.

I felt a flash of triumph.

This wasn't an ordinary score; this was the biggest payday of our lives!

The cabinet was locked.

Bobby flinched as I smashed the glass. The sound was sharp and violent in the hush of the house. He looked at the rifles like they were cursed, but he took one when I shoved it into his hands. I could see it: his struggle between who he was and who he thought he needed to be to keep up with me.

We found car keys on a tray that sat on the dresser, a neat little invitation to leave in style. A Jeep sat outside, silver, catching the moonlight. It was too enticing for us to resist. We were running now, hearts pounding, our world focusing down to a single mission: escape.

We hopped into the Jeep.

I shouldn't have been able to drive it, and neither should he.

We weren't old enough, we didn't have licenses, and nobody had ever taught us how to drive.

But before I ran away from home in the sixth grade, I had been sneaking out at 3 a.m. It was easy to steal my mom's car while she slept after a hard night of drinking.

So I was a self-taught driver, learning on the dark rural roads outside Blue Grass at twelve years old.

And looking back now, I'm sure it showed.

But the engine roared to life, and we tore down the driveway.

Bobby sat rigidly beside me, the rifle resting across his lap.

"You good?" I asked, shouting over the wind rushing through the open windows.

He gave me a weak nod; his eyes fixed on the dark road ahead. "I guess," he said.

I didn't need him to be sure. I had enough certainty for both of us. The city blurred past, and for that wild, stolen moment I felt untouchable.

The gravity of what we'd done, of who we were becoming, would hit later. But right then, in the heartbeats between the moment and the consequences to come, all that mattered was the feeling that was roaring in my chest.

It was something like freedom, something like victory, some kind of glory.

I knew this wasn't the end. This was just the beginning.

8

DAD

I was just fourteen years old.

Life threw me a curveball I didn't see coming. It wasn't the system, or some court order this time.

It was a girl's mom, a woman who barely knew me, but who saw enough to know I needed help. She decided, in the way that some moms do, that it was time for me to reconnect with my father. By then, I was more animal than boy. I'd been hardened by the streets, skittish, quick to fight, slow to trust. I was the kind of kid you crossed the street to avoid, not the kind you tried to bring home. But she did. And then she tracked my dad down.

He was in the small town of Anamosa, Iowa, a sleepy place surrounded by rolling farm fields. She set up a meeting.

The first time my dad and I reunited, the first time I truly *saw* him, was at a Hardee's in the roughest stretch of the Five Points neighborhood in Davenport. The smell of fry grease and old cigarette smoke clung to every surface, and low conversations inside mixed with the occasional outburst from the street outside. I remember standing there, staring at him across a plastic table, feeling a storm of emotions I didn't have the language for: anger, hope, resentment, confusion. Here he was – the man whose blood ran through my veins – but he felt like a stranger.

I don't remember what we said to each other. But somehow, against all odds, my father convinced me to go home with him. Maybe it was the way he looked at me, like he wanted to fix something. Maybe it was because, deep down, I was still a kid who just wanted a place to belong. A week later, in a burst of optimism or desperation or maybe both, he enrolled me back in school.

It was a disaster from the jump. I hadn't set foot inside a classroom in nearly two years. I didn't know how to sit still anymore, how to raise my hand, how to be a student. I wasn't just behind academically, I was behind in everything: Social rules, trust, how to make friends. I didn't know how to act around other kids who had rules, routines, and parents packing their lunches. I was something else entirely now: wild-eyed, twitchy, untrusting. Feral.

The teachers didn't know what to do with me. My classmates didn't either. I could feel it in the way they watched me, knowing I was troubled, suspecting I might be dangerous. They moved through the days as dancers who knew the choreography: homework, hand-raising, lunch lines, inside jokes. But I stood there like a foreigner without a map or a guide. Every bell that rang and every stern look from a teacher only increased the distance between their world and mine. Life on the streets had carved things into me that couldn't be smoothed out by a few weeks of normalcy. I was a boy with no blueprint, trying to build a life from scraps. My dad had good intentions by taking me in and enrolling me in school.

Unfortunately, good intentions do not always produce good results.

I didn't belong in school, and I knew it the minute I stepped through its heavy double doors. My whole way of life had been created by years of surviving without walls or structure. I recoiled at the idea of permission slips and hall passes. The expectation to ask before moving or to nod obediently at orders barked from behind a desk felt laughable (and infuriating). I didn't know how to submit, and worse, I didn't want to.

It wasn't rebellion for rebellion's sake; it was the way I'd learned that life worked. For me, following someone else's rules meant getting hurt. Now, even the well-worn, broadly accepted structure of public school felt like a trap to me.

I resented my father more with each passing day. His attempts at forcing me into this rigid, orderly life felt like one betrayal after another. I didn't want to be a project, a broken boy who needed to be repaired. I didn't want to be a stray dog to be trained. I felt like I was who I was because the world had made me this way, and he was part of that world. He didn't understand that. Couldn't. Wouldn't. In his mind, if I didn't fit neatly into the mold he had envisioned, there was only one solution left: Remove the problem.

And the problem for me was this: Junior high felt small and suffocating, rules stacked on rules, teachers watching for the next mistake. So I left with two friends, one a boy, the other a girl, the three of us drifting away from the building like smoke, laughing too loud, pretending the day belonged to us.

Anamosa is a beautiful town on the Wapsipinicon River, where the land breaks open into yellow limestone cliffs. I loved those cliffs. I loved how climbing them demanded your full attention, how there was no pretending when you were hanging onto rock and dirt, fingers aching, heart thumping.

Down by the softball fields there was a tall cliff, maybe seventy-five feet, the kind that made you feel brave just for standing near it. That was where we went, scrambling up, daring each other to climb higher, the town shrinking below us.

What I didn't know is that my dad had arranged for me to be arrested at school and taken to a youth center that day. It was supposed to happen quietly, efficiently, one more attempt to interrupt the spiral I was already in. But I was not at school when the police arrived. So instead of walking down the hallway and finding me at a desk, there were squad cars combing the town, police looking for me.

They found me halfway up that cliff.

I remember looking down and seeing the police and sheriff cars, seeing their uniforms, hearing their voices, calm but urgent.

"C'mon down, Kyle, take it slow, don't do anything stupid."

I climbed down, every movement suddenly heavy with eyes watching me.

The second my feet hit the ground, I ran.

It was pure instinct, not thought, not courage, just the animal part of me that believed escape was always the answer. I made it maybe a hundred yards before they swarmed me. Hands grabbed my arms, my shirt, my future, and just like that the running stopped.

The sheriff who put me in his car surprised me. He was calm, almost gentle, the kind of cool that does not need to prove itself. Instead of driving straight out of town, he turned toward the cemetery on the edge of Anamosa.

He stopped the car.

He got out.

He opened my door.

He let me out.

He stood next to me, and said, "Let's go for a walk."

As we walked among the headstones, he pointed out the dates, the names, kids my age who never got older.

This deputy was trying to give me a picture, trying to show me where this road could end.

He tried, but it did not land. My mind was too distorted, too immature, too wrapped up in itself to grasp what he was offering. I nodded, maybe rolled my eyes inside, already somewhere else. But looking back now, I love his heart. I love that he tried. I love that he saw a kid worth slowing down for.

He took me back to the car, I got in the back, and he drove us to Cedar Rapids, about forty minutes away. The drive felt longer than it was. He didn't have much to say after our walk through the graveyard.

I wasn't surprised that my dad had called the cops on me.

Hurt, yes. But surprised? Not even a little bit. I'd been expecting it almost since our time together began. A cold knot of inevitability had been tightening in my gut for weeks.

Knowing this day was coming had been like being tied to the tracks and watching a train coming down them.

But it wasn't a train. It was a sheriff's car, and it hadn't run me over, it had picked me up to deliver me here.

The Linn County Juvenile Facility was not what I expected. It was a giant house near downtown. It was not bars and concrete; it was just a crappy old house.

The deputy escorted me inside, then muttered, "Good luck" as he turned and left.

The door clicked shut behind him. I stood there for a moment, taking it all in. The walls were sterile, blank white; fluorescent lights buzzed overhead. Every footstep, every sound echoed off the hard linoleum floor. It didn't even faze me. I didn't expect comfort. I didn't expect anything.

Things were different for me now. I was officially a ward of the state, a title that stripped away any possibility of belonging to a family that I might have felt. The streets had been cruel, but at least they were honest. This new world, with its fake smiles and paper-thin promises, felt far more dangerous because I didn't know how to navigate it.

Looking back, it's strange how quickly my identity was rewritten. One day I was a runaway with a dream of a better life; the next, I was a case file, a cautionary tale, and a burden. It might seem crazy, but being on the streets gave me hope that becoming a kid in the system took away.

I was a ward of the state. That was my new identity.

Inside the facility, I found kids slouched against walls, hunched over tables, or pacing up and down the hall like caged animals. They were my people, even if we didn't know each other yet – a bunch of misfits connected by the things we'd survived.

The staff herded me into a small room with twin beds, a desk, and not much else. My roommate was there, lying flat on his bed, arms behind his head, staring up at the ceiling like he was waiting for it to tell him something. He was probably only a year older than me, but his face was hardened already, suggesting someone much older. He was the first person who really spoke to me.

"I've been here a month," he said, like he was telling me what he had for lunch.

"A month?" I repeated, half laughing. "That's forever."

He chuckled, nodding like he knew something I didn't. "Feels like it. But time moves quicker when you stop thinking about it."

I didn't believe him. Couldn't. At fourteen, a month was an ocean you drown in, not something you floated through. I remember lying awake that night, listening to the mechanical hum of the vents, the occasional thud of a door slamming somewhere down the hall, and thinking, *I won't make it a week here.* The air felt heavy, pressing down on me, making me toss and turn as I itched for a way out.

These places were meant to keep kids like me away from the "good kids." They weren't there to turn us around. They were just training grounds for prison, even if we didn't know it yet. It was just a matter of time before we all ended up there.

The staff tried to keep us busy with chores, group talks, and schoolwork. None of it mattered. Every hour dragged like it was designed to wear you down, to grind the fight out of you little by little. By the third day, I'd had all I could take. By the fourth, I had a plan. It wasn't anything elaborate, but it didn't need to be.

"Come with me," I said.

I barely knew her, didn't even know her name. It didn't matter.

The Linn County youth shelter was just a house in downtown Cedar Rapids.

A crappy old house that the county had a bunch of kids living in.

Slipping out wasn't like breaking out of a correctional facility, it was like walking out the front door.

And that's what we did.

My heart pounded in my chest, but it wasn't fear, it was exhilaration. I was a kid who was raised on risk, and escaping a placement fed me a rush of freedom and relief. We didn't know where we were going, but I didn't care. This reckless freedom was thrilling!

We were running away.

It was fall. The days were warm, but the nights were cold.

We walked until we ended up under a bridge by the Cedar River, just a mile or so from the shelter. I was used to sleeping in places like that – cold, rough, and wild – but this girl wasn't. She shivered next to me, her arms wrapped around herself, struggling to keep warm. I didn't know what to say to her. She was scared, and I could feel it, but I couldn't even process my own manic swirl of thoughts, feelings and fears.

The next day, she talked me into going back to the shelter. I don't know why I listened to her.

She seemed to shrink the moment we walked through the shelter's doors. The air inside felt heavier than before, like even the walls resented us for leaving. Staff members stared at us with tight jaws and narrowed eyes. No one said, "Welcome back." No one asked if we were okay. Instead, they surrounded us with their questions, clipped and cold: *Why did you run? What were you thinking?* I didn't have the language to explain the way that my drive to be free howled inside of me. So I shrugged and muttered the first thing that came to mind: "The voices told me to."

As the words slipped out, I heard how crazy they sounded. But maybe that was the point. Maybe it was easier to let them think I was crazy than to admit that I was desperate to be free.

Their reaction was immediate and clinical. Phone calls were made. Papers were shuffled and forms completed. I was no longer a runaway; now I was a liability, potentially a danger to myself. Within hours, I was transferred out.

The hospital they sent me to wasn't far away, but it might as well have been on a different planet. The bright lights in the psychiatric ward hummed so loudly they made my teeth hurt. The doors didn't click shut here the way they had in the placement. They *clanked* as metal slid against metal, not latching but locking.

Every sound echoed against the walls, hollow and sharp.

I was stripped of everything I had, which was really just the clothes on my back.

I had one pair of underwear, and for whatever reason I was terrified of not wearing underwear. So I never gave them up to be washed, which meant I became a stinky kid.

They let me keep them on, but they took the rest of my clothes and handed me hospital scrubs.

The scrubs came with the suffocating awareness in my soul that no one really saw me as a person anymore. I had become a chart, a problem to manage, a set of symptoms to observe from behind a two-way mirror.

I wondered if it would feel better in the psych ward … safer, somehow.

But it was not better, it was much worse.

In the shelter, at least the other kids wore their pain out in the open, like badges. Here, the pain and hopelessness seeped into our surroundings in quieter, more frightening ways. Blank stares. Sudden screams in the middle of the night. A boy rocking in the corner, whispering to someone only he could see. The nurses walked the halls like wardens, not caregivers, and every hour dragged by. If you cried, you cried into your own pillow, because showing emotion only got you more meds and more isolation. I kept my head down. I counted the tiles on the floor. I tried not to feel the crushing truth pressing down on my chest: I was trapped, and nobody was coming to save me.

Days blurred into nights, and nights into something even darker. In that psych ward, it took little time for freedom to become something abstract that I could only half-remember from an earlier time. Had it ever really existed? Had I ever really been free?

I was in the psych ward for three months as a young teen.

I became so violent there that they moved me to an adult floor.

They moved me so that they had the ability to sedate me if needed; that's something they can't do on the youth floor.

Three months in a psych ward has indelible effects, but it finally came to an end because someone in the system decided that my time there was up.

They kicked me down the line to Toledo.

Toledo was an awful, traumatizing, hardcore boot camp for wayward kids. It was nothing short of abuse, and I became a worse person as a direct result of my thirty days there.

But of all the places I was shuffled through after the psych ward, a little time back home with my dad, a few more petty arrests, a few more short-term placements; none stuck in my mind quite like YRH, Youth Recovery House, in Ames, Iowa. It was supposed to be a placement, a structured program meant to rehabilitate kids like me. The house was run mostly by Iowa State University college students, almost all of them barely older than the residents. They were young, naive, and looking for paychecks or adventure … especially the female supervisors. But no one seemed interested in actually supervising us. Rules were more of a suggestion, enforced when it was convenient. To us, it wasn't a placement at all, it was a playground.

It felt like *Lord of the Flies* dressed up in college sweatshirts. Alcohol flowed freely. Drugs weren't exactly hidden. Romantic entanglements between the staff and the kids weren't just whispered about, they were out in the open everywhere.

To a bunch of broken, angry kids who had seen too much of the other side of life, YRH felt magical, like we had finally stumbled into a world where we weren't always subject to someone else's authority. We were really living … mostly on our own terms.

While the chaos of Youth Recovery House unfolded around me, I found myself at a strange and unexpected crossroads. Amid the swirl of poor decisions and blurred lines, someone somewhere in the system decided I was too far behind to shove back into a traditional school setting. I wasn't surprised.

Sitting still in a classroom, pretending to care about world capitals or algebra equations felt about as natural to me as breathing under water. But what came next was something I hadn't expected: They encouraged me to go after my GED.

Now at fifteen years old, the idea of getting my GED felt like someone opening a strange toolbox, reaching in, and handing me a tool I didn't recognize, let alone know how to use.

Most kids my age were worried about homecoming dates or driver's ed.

Me? I would need a court order just to be allowed to try for this thing called a GED, an alternative to a high school diploma.

I remember the day they sat me down and told me. It wasn't framed like a golden opportunity; it felt like one more thing they could check off their list so they could say they'd "helped" me. But I went for it anyway.

Getting the court order felt more official than anything else in my life up to that point.

It was the first time a judge looked at me and, instead of handing me a consequence, handed me a chance. The papers came through, and before I knew it, I was being driven across town to the local community college, a place that felt like another world to me. It was a world filled with people who hadn't fallen through every crack, who didn't have to claw their way through life just to be seen.

I sat at a worn desk in a small testing room, not expecting to pass the exam. But as I worked my way through the questions, something surprising happened – I knew the answers! Not all of them, and not without some scratching and guessing, but enough. I knew enough of them to keep going, and enough to keep believing, for the first time in a long time, that maybe I wasn't as far gone as I thought.

A glimmer of something hopeful sparked inside of me.

When the results came back, even the staff at YRH seemed stunned. So was I. Somehow, in the middle of all the years of madness, without the structure or encouragement that most kids had, I had pulled something out of myself that no one, including me, had seen coming. I had earned my GED. At fifteen years old, a runaway with little structure and little formal education, had taken the first shaky, improbable step toward something better.

The first step, but there was no guarantee that a second step would come.

9

ESCAPE

I didn't really think much about the staff at Youth Recovery House beyond the fact that they were young and mostly just trying to have a good time like we were. The line between staff and residents was blurry; it was obvious there were no real adults in charge. We were just kids desperate for attention, connection, and anything that felt good: both the counselors and us kids who were placed there.

It was inevitable that boundaries would be crossed. I wasn't looking for anything serious, but then I met Leah. She was one of the student-counselors who had graduated, but she continued to hang around the house. She seemed worldly and wise, even though she was probably just lost and drifting like the rest of us. Our relationship wasn't a secret for long.

At the same time, YRH allowed me to get my first real job. I started bussing tables and waiting tables at a Perkins restaurant just a few blocks from the house. On paper, it looked like progress. But under the surface, everything was a slow-motion disaster. I had no real foundation in me, no character to stand on, nothing that could steady a fifteen-year-old kid who had never been taught how to live. I was soaking up something close to frat boy chaos in a youth shelter, learning all the wrong things. Still, compared to the instability and violence I had lived through to get there, it *felt* like progress. It felt like *freedom*!

Eventually, the inevitable collapse came. When my relationship with Leah was discovered, I was given a choice: testify against her for being involved with a minor or face consequences myself. I refused to throw her under the bus. Loyalty was one of the few currencies I still believed in. My refusal to testify sealed my next sentence: They were sending me to Clarinda Academy, a place I had heard whispered about in foster homes and lock-ups as some kind of correctional boogeyman. I wasn't going to let them send me there.

Before the authorities could pick me up, I bolted. I ran straight into the arms of another YRH staff member, Janie, a girl who had always looked at me a little too kindly, and who was willing to take a risk. We lied to her roommates and told them I was eighteen. For a couple of wild weeks, I lived with her in a cramped college apartment filled with secondhand furniture, while we hoped that we could somehow outrun reality. Predictably, that didn't last long. One afternoon, she handed me a bus ticket to Davenport. There were no long goodbyes. No speeches. Just a tired smile and a nod toward the Greyhound station.

It was bittersweet being back on the streets of Davenport again, back to the life that waited for me when everything else fell apart. It wasn't long before my old friend Bobby found me … or maybe I found him. I can't quite remember. Orphans have a way of finding each other.

Bobby and I had broken into plenty of houses before, so this one – we knew it was a retired cop's place – felt like just another easy mark. It was a modest ranch at the edge of town. The windows were dark, the lawn overgrown, and a rusted mailbox leaned toward the road. It didn't scream "danger" to us; it whispered "jackpot."

Inside, it was as if time had frozen. There were doilies on the end tables, and I noticed a thin film of dust over the knick-knacks. Then we found the guns, stowed in a heavy oak cabinet that might as well have been shining like a neon light. Pistols, a rifle, a shotgun. We grabbed what we could carry and stuffed them into pillowcases we ripped from the beds.

We didn't think about where those guns would end up or whose hands they might pass through. At sixteen years old, we were just playing a game we didn't know the rules to. We also didn't know we were in over our heads.

10

MURDER IN THE FIRST DEGREE

I barely had time to process it all before the hammer came down.

When they arrested me, it didn't feel real. "First-degree murder."

I heard the words, but they floated around the room like smoke, refusing to land on me. I hadn't pulled a trigger; I wasn't even at the scene when the shot was fired. It didn't matter. "Possession. Conspiracy. Accessory."

I had been on the run.

They wanted to take me from YRH to Clarina Academy, and I wasn't having it. I had knocked down the old man who was driving the youth transport van, and I had run.

Once again, I was homeless, living off the spoils of my burglaries.

I was in a crash pad when the cops showed up. They came in quickly, but not with lights blazing. The people who owned the place came to find me because the cops were at the door.

They didn't beat down the door, they just knocked, came in, asked for me.

They cuffed me, and I didn't fight.

I thought they were collecting me for running away from a placement.

I had no idea how much more there was to the story.

They hadn't come to get me because I'd run away from a placement.

They came to get me because there had been a murder.

Bobby and I were barely teenagers, still driven by our impulses, and definitely not by foresight or wisdom. We were still young enough to think that night had some magical power to always forgive us by morning. We moved through neighborhoods like we were invisible.

One of our break-ins changed everything.

Inside the house we had found three guns. Cold and heavy. I took the best one, Bobby took the other two. At the time it felt like loot, like winning. Like power. And we felt clever for getting into the house, finding these guns that had been tucked away, they weren't meant to be in our hands, but here we were, and here they were.

Bobby sold one of those guns to a guy named Mick.

That transaction took minutes.

What followed took a life.

Mick used that gun in a shooting. A little girl died. She hadn't been his target, she just got caught in the crossfire. A child who had nothing to do with our recklessness. Her life ended because of a chain of decisions made by boys who thought they were untouchable.

When the weight of it all came crashing down, Mick told on Bobby.

Bobby told on me. Suddenly my name was written in reports.

That's why the cops were at the door. That's why I was in handcuffs.

I was arrested on first degree murder charges.

I had never pulled a trigger. I wasn't even there.

There is a specific kind of terror that comes when you realize your life can be redefined without your consent. One moment you are a kid who thought he was playing a game. The next moment you are staring at a future shaped by a loss you can never undo, a death you will always carry, and a truth you cannot outrun.

I was taken to a detention center and locked up in a sterile concrete cell, where every hour dripped by like syrup, waiting for a court date that could end life as I knew it.

Then came another blow I never anticipated: My dad was dead.

11

MOM'S ON THE PHONE

I was at one of the scratched stainless steel tables, playing cards with a few other kids, the television murmuring something none of us were really watching. It was just a boring night in the Scott County Detention Center, fluorescent lights humming, time moving in that dull, padded way it always did inside places like that.

Then a guard stepped through the door and said, "ORTH! Kyle ORTH!"

My head snapped up so fast my chair scraped the floor. Nighttime call outs were never good. After dinner, after count, after the doors had made their final clicks, you didn't get pulled unless something was wrong. New charges. Detectives. Or worse, something that would make the rest of the unit think you were snitching. My mind raced through every possibility, my stomach tightening, my chest getting hot. I could already feel the eyes on me as I stood up.

I followed the guard down the hallway. They didn't take me to an office or an interview room. They took me to a padded cell. That alone made my heart start pounding harder. The door opened, soft walls glowing under white light, and a phone was handed to me. Then the door closed behind me, sealing me inside with nothing but the buzz of electricity and my own breathing.

It was my mom on the line. I hadn't talked to her in years. Her voice didn't warm up or ease into it. She didn't circle the truth. She told me straight, in no uncertain terms, that my dad was gone. His second wife had called my mom. He had gone in for a gastric bypass. His heart gave out during the surgery. That was it.

The words didn't land all at once. They just sat there, heavy and unreal. I remember staring at the padded wall in front of me, tracing the seams with my eyes, waiting for something to make sense. I don't remember crying. I don't remember saying much of anything. The conversation was over in less than three minutes. Then the line went dead.

Numbness rushed in. My body had decided this was too much and flipped a switch.

A few minutes later, the door opened again. A guard told me I'd need to strip down and put on a green suicide prevention suit. It was thick and awkward, like a bulletproof vest designed to erase your shape. It definitely erased your dignity. They called it a turtle suit.

I was told I'd be sleeping in that padded room until a psychologist cleared me, a few days at least. Isolated. No cards. No books. No distractions. Just white light and soft walls and endless time.

I had just lost my dad. And now I was alone. In a padded cell. In a turtle suit.

At first, there was still that numbness, a strange calm that felt almost like floating. But with nothing to occupy my mind, no noise except the hum of the lights, the sadness eventually found me. I curled into the fetal position and bawled. It came slow and then all at once. A deep, aching sadness, followed by a loneliness so deep I felt it in my entire body. I curled in on myself on the padded floor, the suit stiff and unfamiliar, the room too bright, too quiet.

I was terrified.

I was completely alone.

12

GRAVESIDE

"Complications from surgery," they said. Complications. That word felt so cruel. *Complication* didn't begin to scratch the surface of what hearing those words, and the treatment that followed, had done to me.

They let me go to the funeral, but not like a son should. Like a criminal. I felt like I looked like Hannibal Lecter. I was wearing an orange jumpsuit. Steel cuffs around my wrists. Leg cuffs around my ankles. Sheriff's deputies flanked me on either side. Military police in front of me and behind me. I remember stepping out of the prison van, the cold autumn air penetrating the thin fabric of the jumpsuit, as faces turned toward me with a mixture of pity and disgust. My family barely looked at me. Maybe I was already a ghost to them. Maybe they were ashamed of me, embarrassed.

Back in the detention center, there was no opportunity to grieve. I didn't know the people. Everybody there had their own issues to deal with. It was isolating. It was jail. It was not home. It was not normal.

But the nights were the worst. That was when the walls would close in, when the what-ifs would slither under the door and wrap around my throat. What if I had stayed in school? What if I had just listened to someone – *anyone* – along the way? Would I be here? Would I still be staring down a future in prison?

Regret is a cruel and useless companion. It keeps you company, sure, but it paralyzes you. I couldn't change what I'd done. I couldn't undo the chain of choices that had dragged me here. All I could do was survive.

Eventually, the truth about what had happened came to light. I hadn't fired the fatal shot. There wasn't enough evidence to say I had. The murder charge crumbled into lesser offenses, and instead of spending decades in prison, I was sent to Clarinda Academy, the place I'd been threatened with a year earlier when I had run away from YRH.

I'd only heard whispers about it back then. Clarina Academy certainly wasn't freedom, but it wasn't the doom of decades in prison. Somehow, God had thrown me a lifeline. And in some small, battered corner of my heart, hope flickered again, dim and fragile. But hope was alive, and maybe I still had a shot at something more, something better.

Maybe.

13

SUFFERING CLARINDA

Clarinda Academy was hell. There's no other way to put it.

Clarinda Academy was a place you survived by disappearing inside yourself. From the moment I stepped through the iron doors on the main building, the air felt like it carried the weight of a hundred years of suffering and sadness. The walls were yellowed and cracked, stained. The ceilings were high and hollow, the fluorescent lights were harsh and cold.

The staff operated under the guise of "structure," but what they really enforced was submission. Wake up at 5 a.m. Physical training until your muscles screamed. Chores. Schoolwork that was meaningless, designed to control, not to educate.

We were marched everywhere – no talking, no looking around, eyes straight ahead, hands at our sides. We attended endless group sessions where you were required to confess your "faults" and weaknesses to the others. If you didn't cry hard enough or seem sorry enough, the staff would start over. They'd needle and humiliate you until you broke down the way they wanted. Any flicker of defiance was swiftly extinguished.

Clarinda Academy was part of America's for-profit prison enterprise.

Troubled kids from around the U.S. were sent to this facility in Iowa, so even though I was from Iowa, I was with kids from across the country.

At night, the building groaned and whispered. It was an old place, and the noises didn't sound natural. Sleep didn't come easily, not because of the creaky beds or thin, scratchy blankets, but because you knew that tomorrow would be another day of the same mind games, the same drills, the same hollow-eyed stares from other troubled kids, trapped and beaten down. Sometimes you'd hear someone down the hall sobbing quietly. Sometimes you'd hear fists pounding a mattress in rage, but you knew it was all a waste of energy, futile.

The cruelest thing about Clarinda wasn't the physical hardship, although that was real enough. It was the way they convinced you, little by little, that you deserved this punishment, that you were broken beyond repair, that you were unwanted, that hope was foolish.

Looking back now, I can see it clearly: Clarinda Academy was never about rehabilitation. It was about containment. About keeping society comfortable by stashing its unwanted children out of sight and out of mind. I survived, but not because of anything they gave me or taught me. I survived because, deep inside, a stubborn spark refused to be extinguished.

Of all the places I had been, Washington Hall at Clarinda Academy haunted me the longest, like a recurring nightmare. The building itself looked like it had been designed for suffering. There were long, sterile hallways, ceilings that hung low, like a constant threat. The windows were too small to let in much light, as if hope itself was being rationed. The linoleum floors were dulled by decades of wear. Every surface felt hard, cold, and indifferent. Our rooms were just four walls containing mattresses. No pictures, no personal touches, no color; just bare concrete and white paint. Lying awake at night, staring up at the ceiling, I wondered if the building could hear our thoughts or feel our loneliness.

"Correctional" routines were rituals of degradation dressed up as discipline. Days blurred into each other under the constant threat of punishment. If you breathed wrong, moved wrong, or looked wrong, you were punished swiftly, and usually without explanation. I can still remember the bristles of a brush burning against my knuckles as I scrubbed grout lines on my hands and knees, not because the floors needed it, but because breaking us down into obedient shells was the real goal. It wasn't about learning responsibility. It was about removing any last shred of defiance.

There were moments when the abuse tipped from psychological to physical so quickly you barely had time to register it. The staff gave the abusive actions names like "control techniques" or "restraint protocols," but we knew better. It was violence, plain and simple. Violence sanctioned and justified by the lie that it was for our own good. I remember the smell of the rubber mats they would throw you onto, the rough scrape of the floor against your skin when they "took you down," and the way the world would narrow to just the sound of their shouting in your ear. And worst of all, the way nobody ever apologized afterward. There was no acknowledgment of harm. Just the expectation that you would get up and keep marching in line as always.

What they couldn't understand was that we were so deeply wounded long before we arrived. They treated our trauma like misbehavior, our survival instincts like rebellion.

The taxpayer expects that these places create stability, maybe even redemption. Instead, in places like Washington Hall, what you learned was how to harden yourself in ways you didn't even know were possible. I learned to expect cruelty. I learned that being in control meant being cruel.

It's almost surreal to think that a place designed to help broken kids could be so adept at breaking them down further. Clarinda Academy didn't heal anyone. It taught us that trust was foolish, that authority was a threat, and that the only one you could count on was yourself.

Unlike the others, I didn't have the rigid schedule of schoolwork to hide behind. I had already earned my GED, an achievement that should have meant something, but in Clarinda, it only meant longer hours under the whip of "physical training." The barking orders, the endless drills designed for dominance over us. Push-ups until your arms gave out. Running until your legs buckled.

Then sitting in circle therapy, not to be healed, but to be monitored, your confessions stored away like ammunition, waiting to be used against you.

We didn't make friends; we made shallow alliances of convenience, because to trust someone was to offer up a part of yourself that could be shattered at any moment. Vulnerability wasn't seen as human; it was seen as weakness, and weakness was mercilessly exploited. We learned to keep our eyes forward, our mouths shut, and our hearts locked tight.

Looking back, it's staggering to realize how many lives passed through those gates only to leave worse than they came. Hundreds, maybe thousands. Each one a life that was supposed to find redemption but instead found deeper wounds.

When I think about Clarinda Academy, I think about how it stripped away the delicate layers of trust, self-worth, and hope we might have had when we arrived. It turned kids like me into shadows of ourselves. Real laughter became a foreign language.

By the time I left Clarinda Academy, I'd been stripped down to the bone and hollowed out. But when I stepped out of those gates for the last time, my head was high even if my heart was battered.

Clarinda Academy was not a place of healing for me, it was a place of harm. I can't say it was the worst thing I ever experienced in my life, but it was definitely a deep, painful mark that I carry to this day.

The anger I carried when I walked out of Washington Hall was not a flickering flame, it was a roaring inferno. And for a long time after, that fiery fury fueled everything I did. I vowed to myself that I would never again let anyone make me feel that powerless. Not the system, not the world, not anyone.

Leaving, when the time would finally come for each of us, was stepping into the world with a mind already set against it, carrying invisible scars that shaped everything we became during our time there.

Clarinda Academy finally closed, after years of pressure that steadily hollowed the place out. Officially, the operators said enrollment had dropped too low to keep the facility running.

Fewer boys were being sent there. The beds were emptying. On paper, it was a simple business decision.

But there was more to the story, and I had been part of it. Clarinda Academy had been under a growing cloud of scrutiny. States and counties that once sent young people there withdrew their placements after complaints mounted. Complaints that made their way through the system: concerns about safety, about care, about the practices that I lived through that were more punitive than rehabilitative. Watchdog reports raised alarms over the use of physical restraints and the treatment of vulnerable youth. Families, advocates, and regulators made the academy harder to sustain. The company that operated it, already facing national criticism over similar facilities, began closing programs across the country. In 2021, the doors shut with a brief announcement and an emptied campus, but it had already done to me what it did to so many others.

It took a kid from an abusive childhood, a runaway, and it hardened me, filled me with rage, taught me leadership by cruel, brutal control, made me physically strong through endless workouts, and then sent me out into the same world that you live in.

14

PAYDAY

There was no one waiting for me outside those bleak fences. No joyful reunions. No plans. No roadmap. Just me, standing there with everything I owned shoved into a plastic bag, blinking in the sunlight like an animal that had been captured and was now being relocated, released back into the wild. I didn't have a home to return to, no mom, no dad, no safety net waiting with open arms.

The only lifeline I had was a girl named Sarah. We had known each other when I'd briefly gone to school in Anamosa when I was living with my dad. She was a classmate and girl I dated, and somehow, through all the chaos, we had stayed in touch. She convinced her parents to let me crash with them, just for a while. It was charity, and it felt like a miracle.

I also had something else.

I had no idea it was coming.

Apparently, my dad had been receiving Social Security disability payments before he died.

Since I was listed as his dependent, I was entitled to a back pay lump sum.

I barely understood it, but suddenly I had $28,000.

At seventeen years old, a check like this felt like the golden ticket to a brand-new life.

One day I was broke, just out of juvenile detention, and the next, I was flush with more money than I had ever seen in my life.

For a seventeen-year-old kid like me who had mostly been homeless or incarcerated, $28,000 felt limitless. Boundless. Like the whole world was finally mine to conquer!

And so, I did what seventeen-year-old me thought freedom looked like: I bought a car.

I didn't have a driver's license, hadn't even thought about getting one, but that didn't matter. I needed a way to get moving, to *go*. So I put the car in Sarah's name, handed over the cash, and for the first time in my life, I felt the thrill of holding a set of car keys in my hand.

I hadn't bought a car. To me, I had just acquired power. Potential. Possibility.

Next came an apartment in Cedar Rapids. It was a run-down unit in a part of town most people avoided after dark, but it was *mine*. Convincing a landlord to rent to a minor wasn't easy. In the end, I paid the entire lease up front, twelve months' rent in cash, which was probably the only reason he handed me the keys without asking any more questions.

After that, things devolved fast.

Cheap liquor.

Music blasting from stolen speakers.

Staying up until sunrise with people who barely knew my name but called me "brother" anyway.

Girls.

Parties.

Blurry nights.

Not blurred lines … no lines.

The emotions that had driven so much rage and violence were pushed down in favor of this euphoria. Newfound freedom and money made a wild teenage party. I was a kid who wanted to have fun, and now for once I'd get to be the guy who could be known for always throwing the party.

Drugs became a factor. Not addiction, but "designer drugs." Party drugs. Ecstasy. Pills. Stuff like that.

And it's wild. One night I passed out, and my friends thought I was dead. They rolled me up in a rug and threw me in a dumpster. I woke up in the morning … *not dead.*

Do you know how hard it is to roll yourself out of an area rug in a dumpster!?

It was that kind of chaos.

I spent money like it would never run out, like I could outrun the consequences forever.

For six wild months, I lived like a reckless, foolish king with no throne, no kingdom, and no clue. But after years of being controlled, monitored, and beaten down, the chaos was intoxicating. It was *mine.*

I had ripped the metaphorical leash from my neck, and I wasn't about to put it back on.

But of course, chaos has a cost.

The money dried up, because even though $28,000 felt like millions to me, it's not millions. It's amazing it lasted as long as it did.

One day I was paying cash for rounds of drinks for strangers, and the next, I couldn't pay my electric bill.

That's when the old familiar instincts kicked in. Survival mode. The kind of instincts that didn't ask questions about right and wrong, only about what it would take to make it through the next day. That's when I turned back to what had worked in the past: Burglary.

It started small. A house here, a house there, then another. A guy named Mark and I became literal partners in crime. We were reckless, careless, and we were making quick cash.

We moved through quiet neighborhoods like shadows, checking windows, doors, drawers, closets; shoving stolen goods hastily into pillowcases. We told ourselves a thousand lies to justify our actions.

These people would be fine, that a flat-screen TV or a jewelry box wasn't life or death, they had insurance, they'd get their stuff back, we needed it more than they did. But beneath what we told ourselves, I developed a gnawing awareness that we were taking more than possessions. We were robbing strangers of the one thing that can't be replaced once it's stolen: a sense of security.

What characterized my life was mania. Pure, unadulterated mania.

I was an undiagnosed bipolar and nothing triggered it more than large sums of money.

I was unhinged, unbridled, torrential mania in teenage form.

So the neighborhoods we hit began to run together, and the more we stole, the easier it became. All in a day's work, just going to the office.

Each successful job increased our confidence – our recklessness – a little more. We stopped casing places beforehand. We stopped checking to see if anyone was home. We got sloppy.

How long it went on is hard to recall. It was more than six months, less than a year.

Burglaries became routine, and they gave me the money for the life that I wanted to live. I had built an entire identity around it. I had no real job and no prospects of having one, but somehow, I had created a world that looked, from the outside, like success. I had the clothes, the electronics, the furniture, the kinds of things kids my age could only dream about. And it wasn't just about having nice things. It was about the *image* they gave me. I was the guy everyone wanted to be around, the one throwing parties, the one with the keys to my own place.

The homeless boy had his own place.

In the middle of the madness, when every day was a hunt to find something else to steal, something else to pawn, some new way to fuel the fast life I couldn't really afford, I met Daisy. I was seventeen, riding a high I didn't realize was leading me straight off a cliff. Daisy was probably fifteen, though she carried herself like someone who'd lived longer and experienced more.

She was from Anamosa, and I had history there.

Anamosa isn't just known for being a small town in Eastern Iowa, it's also known for having a federal penitentiary.

Daisy's house sat across the street.

Maybe a premonition.

Daisy was different than the girls I usually chased after, the ones who got swept up in the flash of stolen money, the cars, and the wild nights. She didn't care about any of that. She wasn't impressed by the gold chain around my neck or the way I threw money around. She wasn't about fast living. Daisy was direct and genuine. There were no pretenses with her; what you saw was what you got. She wore ripped jeans and heavy metal band tees, usually something dark and loud like Insane Clown Posse. She hung around older guys who looked like they lived in their parents' basements, with oversized JNCO jeans, thick black eyeliner, and metal stuck through their eyebrows and lips. I didn't fit into that scene at all, not even a little, but somehow, with her, it didn't seem to matter.

We were from two different worlds, Daisy and me.

I was obsessed with speed. Fast cars, fast money, fast living, and she moved through life with a slow, deliberate beat that you couldn't rush even if you tried.

But there was something about her that drew me in. For being so young, she had an independence I envied. No one seemed to be watching her, telling her no, pulling her strings like they did with every other kid I knew. She had carved out a little corner of the world where she made her own rules. I didn't know how to do that. I only knew how to run.

We didn't exactly "date" the way most people would describe it. It was looser than that. We'd meet up here and there, sometimes in a parking lot, sometimes at house parties where the music shook the walls and the smell of cigarettes hung in the air. Our connection was casual and undefined, but it was real in a way few things were for me back then. She had a trustworthiness about her, something grounded that I couldn't find in the people I partied with or the people I stole with. When I was around Daisy, there was no pressure to impress, no need to be "on." I felt a strange kind of peace when I was with her.

Looking back, I can still see her, leaning against a cracked brick wall, the glow of a cigarette lighting her face in orange, her eyes steady, unreadable, but kind. Almost everything in my life was built on lies, but Daisy was one of the rare things that felt honest. And maybe that's why, even in the midst of my worst decisions, I kept going back to her. Not because she was a part of the chaos, but because she wasn't.

She invited me to church with her family. To say that it was not a fit is an understatement.

I had been to church before. I was not hostile to it.

But my mind, back then, was never still. It lived in a kind of permanent sprint, like an engine stuck in the scary-high RPMs. I was manic, vibrating. Survival had narrowed my world into a tight tunnel, and everything outside of that tunnel existed only as noise.

So when people spoke about God, it reached me only in my peripheral. I heard there was a man named Jesus, that He offered something like rest, forgiveness, a different way to live. I caught fragments of it the way you catch parts of a conversation from another room, recognizable but indistinct. My inner world at that time in my life was too loud, too fuzzy to lock in on what was being offered. It was not rejection, it was incapacity. I was not saying no; I simply did not know how to stop long enough to say yes.

Meanwhile, my apartment was the epicenter of the chaos, the place where the music was always loud, where there was always beer in the fridge, and where nobody ever asked the wrong kinds of questions. Kids from all over would show up, people I barely knew, drawn by the rumors of endless parties and no adults around to kill the buzz. They came to escape their lives for a night, and I let them. I loved being the one who could offer that. It made me feel important, powerful. But there was a rot setting in, a sick reality that every bottle we opened, every game we played, every meal we ate was being bought and paid for by violating someone else's sense of security.

I was the chief thief in a den of robbers.

The truth was, I couldn't stop if I wanted to. The rush of breaking into homes, the quick jolt of adrenaline when I popped a lock or slipped through a back window – it was a drug. More than the cash, more than the lifestyle, *that* was what had its hooks in me. I'd sit at a party, music blasting, bodies moving around me, and all I could think about was which house I'd hit next. I scanned neighborhoods in my mind the way a gambler eyes a deck of cards, always wondering where my next score would come from. Breaking in wasn't just my livelihood, it was my identity. Daylight was for burglaries; nightfall was for parties. And around and around the wheel spun, faster and faster.

But at seventeen, with a broken moral compass, a hard heart, and an intoxicating life, I didn't have the capacity to slow down and see it. I just pressed harder on the gas, burning through everything in my path.

And then reality – swift, brutal, and unapologetic – stepped in.

Sarah was my accomplice.

She stayed in the car.

We didn't bother to wonder why there were two flagpoles out front or why the mailbox was filled with official-looking mail. We were too arrogant, too stupid, and too desperate.

The sun was high and hot in the clear blue sky that summer day.

Iowa's characteristic humidity made us sweaty, sticky.

Sarah's grip was tight on the steering wheel, her knuckles pale, as she drove down a gravel road toward the acreage.

I'd always preferred daylight for jobs like this. There weren't shadows to hide in, but there was less chance of someone being home, and the odds of running into trouble were lower. I knew what I was doing. I always thought I did.

Sarah didn't say much as we neared the house, but I could see the tension in her body, the stiffness in her shoulders. She was nervous. I could feel her glance at me when she thought I wasn't looking. She was wondering, like I always wondered about people, what I was thinking. What I was planning.

A long gravel drive curved up toward the house, framed by clusters of trees that almost created a barrier between the mansion and the rest of the world. It was a massive place. Two stories, large windows, a front porch that wrapped around to the side. The kind of house that just screamed "rich."

I slid out of the car without a word, the door barely making a sound as I opened and closed it. Sarah stayed behind the wheel, watching. She wasn't a stranger to this kind of thing but today was different. The house was bigger, the stakes higher. I could sense her hesitation.

I turned toward the house and moved toward the front steps. I had a plan.

She drove a half mile away to watch for the cops or the homeowner.

My job was to get in fast, make it quick.

There was no one around; I was sure of it. It was the middle of the afternoon, and most people weren't home. They were working, living their normal lives, while I was here doing what I did.

I slid my BB gun out from my waistband. It was always a simple thing to shoot through a window, just enough to jolt the lock and get it loose. A soft pop, and it was done. It was quick and efficient, the way I liked it.

I slid open the window and climbed through, landing with a quiet thud on the hardwood floor inside. The smell of old wood hit me immediately, a stark contrast to the humid summer air outside. The house was silent except for the hum of the air conditioner. I stood up, straightened my shirt, and took a moment to assess the layout. I always went to the master bedroom first. It gave me the lay of the land, a chance to clear the rest of the house in my mind. And, of course, that's where the good stuff was: Jewelry, cash, guns. The things that made it worthwhile.

I moved with precision, quickly stripping the pillowcases off the bed; they would be ideal for carrying the loot. Using pillowcases had become a signature move for me. It was part of my system, and it always worked. I took what I needed and moved on, never staying too long. Fifteen minutes, I told myself; that was all I needed.

I reached into the drawer of the nightstand and pulled out two small revolvers. I didn't hesitate. They went straight into a pillowcase, and I turned to leave.

It was time to go.

I called Sarah to come back and get me, but my cell phone didn't work.

So I climbed onto the roof. Still didn't work. Out of desperation, I climbed back inside and used the home phone.

That was a mistake.

There is no right house to break into, but there are definitely wrong ones.

This one belonged to the Jones County District Attorney.

Of all the houses in all of Iowa, we picked his.

Not on purpose, just looked like a good mark.

It wasn't bad luck, something like this was bound to happen sooner or later.

The thing is, I didn't know right away. I did a few more burglaries, I got caught up in a few more debacles, and on the way back to my apartment from one, a car was trailing me. It turns out, it was an unmarked police car.

To this day, I don't know where all these cars materialized from, but instantly we were swarmed with police. A helicopter appeared out of nowhere.

The officers smashed out the windows of my car and slammed me to the ground so fast, and with no mercy.

There is hurried conversation. The Feds are there. The city. The county. Once the Feds find out that I'm a minor, they don't want the case.

The cops stuffed me in the back of a cruiser and take me to the sheriff's department.

I'm back in custody, and so is Sarah.

Sarah's only real crime was caring about me at a time when I had nothing to offer anyone. She and her family took me in when I had nowhere else to go, fed me, gave me a couch, gave me a place to breathe. They treated me like a human being long before I remembered how to act like one. And because of that, because they opened their door to a kid who was already unraveling, she got pulled into the blast radius of my choices.

After the burglary arrest, her name got written on reports she never should have been part of. She was charged as an accomplice even though all she had ever done was try to help someone she cared about. She had no record, no history of trouble, no pattern of bad decisions. And maybe that is why the courts saw the truth of who she was. They gave her probation, a small mercy that felt like grace breaking through the mess I had created.

I look back now and realize how twisted my thinking had become. I believed I was helping her by involving her in the hustle, as if dragging someone into my chaos was a form of loyalty. I was so far gone that harm and help looked like the same thing to me. She was good. I was not. And the guilt of pulling her into something she never deserved has stayed with me in a quiet, steady way.

She walked away with a future still intact. I thank God for that. And I carry the regret of ever letting her name get tied to mine during the dark abyss of my life. Her only mistake was opening her door to someone who had forgotten how to stay out of trouble. Her heart was good. I was the one who brought trouble.

And not just to her. I was involved with a number of girls at that time.

It was a manic season.

Going to jail didn't end it.

15

TRAPPED

'm sitting in my cell.

I remember all that led to me being here.

Sarah and I had only been involved in a couple of burglaries together, the DA's house being one of them. It was usually Mark who was with me. Mark had been my main partner house after house, week after week. The DA's place was the one that eventually brought all the attention and news headlines. There were months and dozens of burglaries between the high-profile break-in and the day it all finally came to an end.

The day Mark and I got arrested was another sizzling summer day, with the sun like a white-hot blast furnace baking the earth beneath it. County Home Road, north of Cedar Rapids, stretched ahead of us like a taut ribbon, endless and empty, the asphalt shimmering in the summer heat. My Mercury Cougar purred down the blacktop as he clenched the steering wheel. We'd just finished another house. Two teenagers according to our years, made older by our life's experience. This was just another job. By then, it was routine.

The silence inside the car wasn't awkward. We'd shared in countless crimes; we also shared a silent understanding. I stared out the window at the cornfields lining the sides of the road, the leaves on the green stalks swaying lazily in the hot breeze. My mind wasn't on the scenery though. It was on the next house. The next score. There was always a next thing waiting.

Suddenly a tightness crawled up my spine, making the hair on the back of my neck stand on end. "Mark," I said sharply, my voice almost a whisper. "You see that?"

He didn't answer right away. He checked the rearview mirror, and his mouth tightened into a hard line. I followed his gaze. At first, I thought it was a trick of the heat, just a ripple in the sky, but then it came into focus: a helicopter. Not a news chopper. The kind that *hunts.*

"What the hell?" Matt half muttered, half shouted, as he pressed harder on the gas pedal. The Cougar surged ahead, picking up speed. But it was already too late.

The helicopter didn't pass. The sound of the blades cut through the thick air, deafening. The thudding of the chopper blades grew louder until it drowned out everything else.

My heart pounded as squad cars suddenly appeared, one ahead of us and another behind, with lights flashing and sirens screaming. It was like they had been lying in wait just out of sight, and now the trap was springing shut on us.

"Get down!" I ordered, but Mark was jerking the wheel, trying to find an escape route. He veered hard to the left but the road was too narrow and the cops were too fast. There was nowhere to run. We were surrounded.

Then – *CRASH!* – the passenger window beside me exploded inward, showering me with shards of glass. The world became a blur of motion and sound. Hands were grabbing me, voices shouting, bodies slamming. I was yanked from the car and thrown to the ground, my breath whooshing out as my chest hit the gritty shoulder of the road.

"Hands behind your back! Don't move!" someone shouted, sharp and merciless.

I tried to obey as rough hands jerked my arms back and slammed on handcuffs, the steel biting deep into my wrists. The taste of blood and dirt filled my mouth; grit from the road scraped against my teeth. The helicopter roared overhead, the noise mixing with the shouts of officers.

"Where's the other one!?" someone demanded, and before I could lift my head, I heard Mark's voice, frantic, cracking.

"I'll talk! I'll talk! Just don't hurt me!" he screamed. "He's got the stuff! The stash! Everything's at his apartment!"

A lead weight dropped in my stomach. I didn't need time to process it. I already knew *it was over.*

Within minutes, I was locked in the back of a squad car and we were on our way. The heat was suffocating inside the back of the cruiser, plastic separating me from the A/C in the front seat. As the sirens wailed around me and the fields blurred as we passed them, I sat motionless, the cuffs still biting into my wrists. For the first time in a long, long time, there was no next move.

16
JAIL

The walls of the Jones County Jail were as harsh and unforgiving as they were intended to be. I'd gone from being the center of my little kingdom, the person everyone called for a laugh, a drink, or a good time, to this: an angry, scared, frustrated figure in a narrow cell. A face in a crowd of strangers. No more friends. No more parties. Just bright accusing lights overhead and the soft clatter of voices from around the jail.

I spent my eighteenth birthday behind bars. The day came and went without any recognition, of course. I couldn't remember the last time anyone made a fuss over me, but this felt different. 18 years old is supposed to be a special birthday. Mine was spent in jail.

I was so sad. I thought I had so many friends. One of them turned on me, testified against me. No letters, calls, visits. Not one. All of these people whom I'd been throwing parties for were just gone from my life. No loyalty, no real friendship.

And until I turned eighteen, every day in jail was a monotonous grind.

Because I was a minor charged as an adult, I wasn't allowed out in the general population which would have given me access to a day room, with things like TVs, board games, card partners. There was no TV or any other distractions in my sparse cell. The meals all tasted like cardboard to me. The never-ending murmur of the guards and inmates made the walls feel even closer than they were. Beside the bed, carved into the wall in shallow marks, were the words *"Look up."*

It wasn't the first time I'd seen them. At first, they'd just been another insignificant detail, part of the cell I couldn't escape. But something about them... *"Look up."* Every time I laid there, staring at the gray ceiling, I traced those words with my finger, as if they held a secret meaning. The cross etched into the center was almost worn away from my repeated touch, but I never gave it the attention it deserved. I didn't know what it meant, and I didn't really care. I couldn't see past my own anger and despair.

From the narrow window of my cell, stretching across the horizon, I could just make out some rooftops of Anamosa, a town I had once roamed freely. Now my view of it was reduced to glimpses between concrete and steel. And there, almost laughably close, I could see a little house with weather-beaten siding and a sagging porch that I recognized instantly. Daisy's house. Of all the places to end up locked away, it was a cruel irony that I landed within sight of the one girl who had made me feel – even if just briefly – like something more than the mess I had become.

I sat on the edge of the slab they called a bed, squinted through the grimy window, memorized the shape of the street signs, and traced the cracks in the sidewalks with my eyes, until finally I made out her address. Something inside me stirred, something that hadn't felt alive in weeks. So I wrote her a letter on a sheet of the thin, off-white stationery they gave us for free. It felt ridiculous at first, clumsy even, like trying to speak a forgotten language. But the words poured out. Half apology, half confession, all yearning. I didn't know if she'd answer. I didn't even know if she still remembered me.

But she did.

Her reply came back folded neatly, tucked inside one of those cheap pastel envelopes you could buy at the dollar store. When I saw my name in her handwriting across the front of the envelope, the whole cell block faded away. For the moment, I wasn't just a number in a jumpsuit. I was a person again.

Daisy became my only thread of connection to the outside world. Her letters were simple, just a few pages telling me about her day, a memory she had, or a song she liked, but they were a lifeline for me. I read them over and over, studying every curve of her handwriting. They were sacred texts. She had no idea what a gift she was giving me: Her letters were a momentary escape from the suffocating isolation that blanketed the jail. Through her, I could taste freedom, I could remember that there was a world out there bigger than the concrete walls and clanging doors around me.

The hearings for my case started, and with them came tension. I knew I was walking a razor's edge. The DA couldn't prosecute me directly, it was his own house, but that didn't stop him from making sure I never forgot his face. He sat at every hearing, rigid in the front row like a monument to my crimes. His eyes tracked my every move, every stumble, every hesitation. He was a living indictment, a grim reminder that my cleverness had its limits.

My manipulations of the truth couldn't erase the damage I had caused.

They brought in a special counsel for my case, someone whose only knowledge of me was a thick file of documents and what he saw in the courtroom: a kid trying hard not to look like he was crumbling. I kept my head down, answered questions with clipped syllables, and let my public defender do most of the talking.

A court case like this involves some amount of coming and going.

The jail is on the top floor of the courthouse, so between hearings, I'd return to my cell.

Each time the heavy wooden doors swung open and I walked in, I felt like a performer stepping onto a stage in a show I hadn't auditioned for. The audience was made up of court staff, victims' families, and the occasional reporter, who watched me like they were waiting for the inevitable.

The DA's silence said what his mouth didn't need to: *You can't outrun what you've done.*

When the courtroom emptied and I sat alone in the holding cell, I could sense his accusation breathing against my neck.

I had spent so long pretending the world's rules didn't apply to me, spent the last year justifying the wreckage I'd left behind, but now even I couldn't deny it.

When the judge finally announced his decision and offered me work release, it was unbelievable.

The sun cracked through the thick storm clouds I'd been living under.

I felt grateful in a way I hadn't known I was capable of feeling.

They were giving me a chance, a real chance! And somewhere deep inside, a boy I thought I'd buried long ago made a vow: *I will not blow this. I will not go back to the darkness I came from.*

I promised myself right there in the courtroom that I would be different.

I would be better. I would leave that version of myself behind.

I didn't know yet how hard that would be, but in that moment, I believed with everything I had left that I could do it.

17

WORK RELEASE

At first, work release felt like someone had opened a window in a room I'd been suffocating in. I'd been under the oppressive thumb of jail for months, so the fresh air of this relative freedom felt amazing.

It felt reckless just to walk down a street unchained, or to sign my name on a paper and be trusted to leave and then return. I told myself I would treat it like the second chance it was, that this time was different, and I would be better. I really believed that … for a few days.

When you walk out of prison, the door closes behind you with a sound that feels final. Steel on steel. A period at the end of a sentence you swear you will never write again.

I had written that sentence and finished it with a firm period five times in my life.

Five times I promised myself, and anyone willing to listen, "This is it!"

This time I will live straight.

This time I will not come back.

And every time, I meant it. There was no deception in my voice when I said it.

No crossed fingers behind my back. I believed myself.

That is the cruel part.

The human mind is good at keeping us alive, but it also betrays us. It forgets pain as soon as the pain stops screaming. Psychologists call it hedonic adaptation. Mothers forget the agony of childbirth and that allows them to have more children. It happens when we get a big raise or promotion. At first, the extra income feels exciting, but over time expenses often rise to match it, and the "extra money" is gone. The new car experience does it too, those early days of pride and enjoyment, but after a while, the car is just "your car," and it no longer brings the same emotional lift.

And in the same way, men like me forget prison.

"Never again" is powerful when you are freezing in a cell.

It is fragile when you are standing under open sky.

Within twenty-four hours of entering work release, my head was already spinning. Old thoughts came rushing back like muscle memory. Shortcuts. Loopholes. Shady schemes dressed up as solutions. I had sworn them off, but they did not need my permission to return.

Here is another truth that hurts to admit. The brain does not associate crime with prison. It associates crime with relief. Prison comes later. Crime comes with release, with money, with control, with escape from pressure. Crime can be fun. Exhilarating. Over time, the brain links the behavior to the immediate payoff, not the eventual consequence. Prison becomes an abstract future. Relief feels urgent and real.

And for men with minds like mine was – manic – that relief isn't a nice-to-have, it's a need-to-have.

So the truth was, my memory for promises, especially ones I made to myself, was short.

The pull of old habits, that furious fire inside of me, and the cruel lessons of my life up to then was just so much stronger than my newfound resolve to be a nice guy in those first days of work release.

At first, it started small, with quick stolen moments.

I was supposed to be on a track: work release job, back to the halfway house, sleep, back to work. A steady, predictable, consistent track. This was what I'd promised myself I would do as I built a new life with the grace I'd been given.

But I found any excuse I could to sneak off, sometimes to meet Daisy, sometimes just to slip back into the shadows of my past life. I was desperate for connection and that old intoxicating feeling of being wanted and important to someone. And Daisy, loyal Daisy, offered that feeling freely, no questions asked. It didn't matter that the cost of her affection was more than I could afford.

We'd go to the mall and hang out. Make out. We'd walk around town. The teenagers you see walking around when you're running errands? That was us.

I was supposed to be at the Village Inn in Cedar Rapids that day, bussing tables and blending into the mundane rhythm of people just living their lives. I signed out from the halfway house with a steady hand, the ink from the pen flowing smoothly across the page even though my mind was already set on something else.

The letters of my signature blurred as I thought about the night ahead. My mind was laying out the thrill and the recklessness that would come. I didn't even make it halfway to work before I veered off course. Bennigan's was calling …

I met a girl there. A couple of drinks in, the quiet voice of reason in my mind, already weak, completely disappeared.

I got drunk and asked myself, "You know what I should do?"

I answered myself fast, "I should go break into something."

An hour later, as I stood in front of the house I'd chosen, I quickly surveyed it: a simple two-story, a white fence, and too many lights off for anyone to be home. The whiskey I'd downed at Bennigan's was already running hot through me. It made the world hazy, like I was seeing it through a fogged window, but the edge of the fog was sharp. This was what I knew. This was what I could control.

I slipped in through the back gate, the metal creaking under my weight. I knew this routine like the back of my hand, though I was a little out of practice. My fingers fumbled with the sliding glass door as I pulled at it the same way I had with similar doors so many times before. But I screwed up. My foot caught on the threshold, and the glass shattered around me. Instantly my leg screamed with intense pain even through the haze of alcohol. The jagged edge of the doorframe had sliced through my jeans and into my skin.

The shock of what had happened didn't register immediately. But then I looked down and saw it – my jeans soaked through, blood flowing out like crazy. The gash was deep. The skin was torn wide open and I could see inside my calf. The whole thing seemed surreal. The sight of the blood jarred me back to reality, but the world started to spin. My torn jeans were grabbing the wound, and each time I moved, it pulled at the flesh. I tried to step back, but my legs gave out and I collapsed to the floor.

The world closed in around me. I realized the house was still quiet. No one had seen me, and no one would until it was too late. I tried to get up, to drag myself out, but the pain hit me again and I collapsed again, my mind slipping away in slow waves.

I barely registered the screech of tires outside or the flurry of activity that followed. Someone had seen. Someone had heard. I have no memory of being loaded into the ambulance or the ride to the hospital. Once there, everything was a blur.

The bright lights above me hummed and I knew I was lying on a table now, but the sensation of my leg and its torn flesh was like a distant dream, too far away to touch. The doctor hovered above me, his words dull and confusing, but I could feel the swift, practiced way his hands moved, trying to stop the bleeding and put me back together. Blood was everywhere. It coated my skin and soaked my clothes and the sheets beneath me. I realized I could be dying, and part of me didn't care.

A nurse was working quickly too, pressing her gloved hands into the gash, trying to stem the bleeding. "Stay with us," she said, her voice distant, calm. I did as I was told.

My thoughts drifted back to the house, to the door, and to the broken glass that had been my undoing. It wasn't supposed to end like this. But then again, nothing in my life ever went as I had planned.

Over the days ahead as I recovered, the familiar fear, anger and despair crept back into my mind. One minute, I was clinging to a frayed rope of second chances, and the next, I was free-falling into a pit of the same pattern of destruction, with nothing but the inevitable consequences waiting at the bottom. I was heading to prison – really heading there this time. There would be no work release, no suspended sentence. Just iron bars and razor wire. I had this coming. It had come.

That's when I got the news: Daisy was pregnant.

18

FATHERHOOD BEHIND BARS

The Linn County Jail smelled of bleach and urine.

That blend of smells lingered in the air no matter how long you were there – you couldn't get noseblind to it.

It was one of those days when the hands on the clock seemed to move in slow motion. Finally, the time arrived, and I shuffled into the visitation room with my hands cuffed tightly behind my back. My orange jumpsuit stuck to my skin, a firm confirmation of where I was. The heavy metal doors clanged shut behind me.

Daisy was already sitting on the other side of the thick glass that separated us. Her eyes were fixed on the floor, and her fingers kept nervously twisting around something in her lap. I stood there for a moment, taking in the situation. It was hard to grasp how I'd ended up here, locked up and separated from everything I knew and cared about, including her.

Her mom, who had been sitting quietly next to her up until that point, not making eye contact with me, gave me a glance that could've been either judgment or understanding – hard to tell – but she didn't say a word.

Her presence was a calm contrast to the tension that was welling up from my gut to my chest.

I sat down in a plastic chair opposite Daisy. The glass between us made us feel farther away than we were; worlds apart instead of inches. I picked up the phone to begin our conversation. Daisy didn't reach for hers immediately. Instead, she dug through her purse, her hands trembling as she searched. I could hear the rustling of paper, the clink of keys, and then, slowly, her hand came up with a small plastic stick.

For a moment I didn't comprehend what it was, but then it hit me. My stomach dropped and all the sound in the room muffled, the world around me became a blurry haze except for what Daisy was holding in her hand.

It was a pregnancy test stick, and you could clearly see a gray plus symbol.

She tucked it quickly back into her purse and for a moment, I thought I might suffocate in the silence. The question I'd been dreading to ask was on the tip of my tongue, but I wasn't ready to ask. Not here. Not now.

But then she picked up the phone.

The idea of becoming a father was an overwhelming swirl of excitement and paralyzing fear. At just eighteen years old, I was heading to prison for the first time while also preparing to "welcome" a child into the world. Daisy was seventeen and still legally a minor, which meant her mom had to accompany her on visits to see me.

I could feel the heaviness settle between us. Her eyes met mine through the glass, and though I couldn't touch her or hold her, I felt her presence as if she were right beside me. She smiled the same smile I had seen countless times. But this one was different too, gentler and softer. It was like she was trying to reassure me even though the world around us had already started to spin out of control.

Then the dreaded words slipped out of my mouth before I could stop them. "Is it mine?" I immediately regretted asking. It felt stupid, a weak attempt to break the silence. But I needed to know.

Daisy didn't react immediately. She just smiled again, that same soft smile that made my heart ache, and then she nodded. "Yeah," she said, her voice steady and calm. "It's yours."

I glanced over at her mom. There was a hint of irritation in her eyes, but she didn't speak. She just sat there, her hands folded neatly in her lap. Maybe she'd been waiting for me to say something a little more profound, but all I could do was sit there, processing it all. A kid. Our kid. My mind spun, but my mouth stayed shut after that.

Daisy smiled again, this time a little wider. "You're gonna be a dad," she said, the words both comforting and terrifying.

The phone pressed harder against my ear, and for the first time since I had been locked up, I felt more trapped than ever.

Her mom shifted in her seat, the tension in the air palpable, but Daisy just sat there, calm, her gaze never wavering from mine.

That's the kind of person she was.

Despite the circumstances, both Daisy and her mother were supportive of me throughout the pregnancy, trying their best to make sure I could be involved, even from behind bars.

19

PRISON

I had seen it portrayed in movies and heard about it on the streets, but nothing could have prepared me for the cold, grim reality of life in prison.

The first time I walked into the Iowa Medical and Classification Center (IMCC) in Coralville, I was barely nineteen and in over my head. I thought I understood fear; it had been a frequent feeling for me my entire life.

But that day, stepping through the gate of IMCC, I felt a terror that was greater than I ever had before. It was like being thrown into a tsunami that could swallow you whole.

I knew juvenile detention, I had known Clarinda.

I knew jail, but this was different. This was prison.

The guards, with their clipped hair and stern faces, herded us like cattle into a small room. They spoke little, only pointed to the concrete floor where a few lines of men were already standing, naked, hands pressed to the cold walls. I was next in line to step into the room, and the knot in my stomach tightened as the reality of where I was hit me like a hammer.

The staff didn't care about modesty. Our feelings were not relevant here.

Our dignity was forfeited when the gavel fell and our convictions were confirmed.

We were guilty men, and what mattered here was one thing: compliance.

A guard barked out commands and pointed at the powder station.

I followed the others, unsure what the hell I was supposed to do.

They handed me a little packet of white powder and told me to "strip it all off" and then smear the powder on. I felt their eyes on me as I slowly removed my clothes and dusted myself with the powder. It was supposed to kill every trace of disease, every germ that could be hiding on me. But all I could think about was how exposed I felt, how naked and vulnerable I was in front of all the other inmates.

I felt like a kid, a shaking naked kid, surrounded by powerful guards and prisoners who were hard, who knew this routine.

I looked at the other inmates, their expressions cold and indifferent, as if this was a ritual they had been through a thousand times. They didn't care that I was standing there trembling, too young for this. Some of them stared at me, sizing me up. No one showed any signs of sympathy. Just dull, lifeless stares.

It was a horrible, degrading, embarrassing experience … and it was terrifying.

We've all heard about what happens in prison, all the jokes about "don't drop the soap," and here we were, naked, my first time naked in a room full of strangers, every one of them convicted of crimes.

This exposure lasted almost an hour.

Finally, we were given orange uniforms, flip flops, and just a moment to put them on.

Two guards marched me down a hallway that smelled of sweat, and that kept my fear ratcheted up as far as it had ever been.

The place buzzed like a hornet's nest ready to burst. Frustration and anger simmered under the surface of every man there, and as I looked at them, each looked like they were ready to jump me the first chance they got.

I was assigned to F Block, and I was shoved into a cell.

I stared at the steel bunk across from me and my chest tightened. I felt small. I was small. It was impossible not to feel like a caged animal. My bones ached with the fear and my hands shook. I tried to calm myself, but I couldn't. Not one bit. I collapsed onto the bunk and tried to come to grips with the fact that this would be my home for the next number of months. At least no one could assault me in my cell.

My body tensed every time I had to leave the safety of my cell to go to the bathroom or grab something to eat, but what I really hated was going to the day room. As men sat and talked or watched TV or dozed there, others circled like hungry wolves looking for prey. They were waiting for a weakness to show so they could make their move. I was young, trying to be just another face in the crowd, but I could feel their eyes on me whenever I passed through the room. They didn't look at me like I was human.

One day, as I passed a group of men sitting at a table playing cards, one of them looked up at me with a smirk. His voice was low, casual, as if he were feeling me out. "Do you have any Irish in you?" he asked, his eyes glinting.

I froze. A chill ran down my spine. "No," I replied, trying to sound unaffected.

"Do you want some?" he said. The words slipped from his lips like a snake, slow and deliberate.

I didn't understand the joke at first, but the men around the table all laughed, their eyes locked onto me. They weren't laughing with me or at a joke. They were laughing at me. I had no idea how to fight back. I was a very scared kid in a world of wolves.

The days dragged on, and I began to learn what it would take to survive in prison. I learned to keep my head down, to blend in, and to avoid making eye contact for too long. The toughest inmates, the ones who had already earned their place at the top of the pecking order, walked around like they owned the place. The rest of us did our best to stay out of their way.

All I wanted to do was call Daisy. I knew that if I could just hear her voice, even for a minute, it would assure me that I was still human, that there was still someone out there who cared. But I was broke; I couldn't afford to buy phone time. I watched other inmates line up to use the phones, laughing or arguing, connecting with people on the outside, and it tore me apart inside. I didn't want much or even need much, just the sound of Daisy's voice to break through the walls that confined me. It felt like too much to hope for.

Weeks turned into months. I felt my mind and my heart hardening, the softness inside me that I'd gained back during my years of freedom slowly giving way to a dispassionate, emotionless, uncaring persona.

The kid I had been so long ago, the compassionate one who had cared about others, about what was right and wrong, about the underdogs in the world was gone again. I learned to steel myself against the taunts, the jabs, the constant reminder that I was an outsider, that I wasn't one of them, not yet.

One of my problems is that I've always found a way to fit in.

20

SENTENCED

At the IMCC, I was assessed and assigned to the Fort Dodge Correctional Facility (FDCF) for my fifteen-year sentence.

When I arrived in Fort Dodge, I had already become a shell of the kid who had first set foot in IMCC. If I thought the classification center had been rough, Fort Dodge proved me naive in the most brutal way. They called FDCF "Gladiator Camp" and it lived up to every bit of that name.

The second I stepped into the prison yard, I felt it. The weight. The aggression. Anger so ever-present you could smell it. Like you could smell blood in the air, like the rage of these men had somehow soaked into the concrete and could never be washed out.

The men here didn't care about who you were or where you came from; they cared about their status among the other inmates, about who was stronger, who could take what they wanted and crush anyone who got in their way.

I thought I had learned how to survive at IMCC, but I hadn't seen anything yet.

My first few months were nothing but survival in a harsher environment than I had ever known.

I found myself in more scrapes than I could count. Within the first three weeks, I was in half a dozen fights. Some I won; some I barely walked away from. Some were over petty things – a look, a word, a shove – but every one of them left a mark on me. Every bruise, every cut, was a reminder of how far I had fallen from the times I'd been given second chances and squandered them.

I wasn't used to fighting. I'd never had to fight. But here, "fighting" was the native tongue. The language of this place was violence.

I quickly learned that any act of kindness was seen as weakness. If you didn't fight, you didn't survive. Simple as that.

One night after lights out, clanging metal woke me sharply.

I tried to see through the darkness, my heart immediately racing, and listened.

It wasn't just a fight this time. It was something worse: the slapping of a padlock swinging from the end of a sock, cutting the air like a whip. That was normal here. I'd seen it happen a few times. Men in a frenzy, beating each other senseless with whatever they could get their hands on. It was all part of the prison culture that we were now trapped in. Violence wasn't something that was done to you, it was something you had to learn to do if you wanted to live. And so, I learned.

One afternoon, after an especially brutal fight, I sat in the corner of the yard, nursing a black eye and a split lip. Blood was drying on my face, and I could feel a sharp pain in my ribs, but what hurt more was realizing how numb I had become. It was like I had shed every piece of my old self, layer by layer, until nothing was left but survival instincts. I'd seen men get beaten down by fists and then get stomped on, their faces smashed into the ground like nothing more than a rag doll, and I hadn't flinched. With my sense of compassion erased, I hadn't thought twice about stepping over their bodies and walking away.

Inside the prison, everything was divided by race: The yard, the cafeteria tables, even who you could talk to. Gangs operated in the open, a constant source of tension among the inmates. It wasn't a question of "if" you'd get approached; it was a matter of "when." The white gangs tried to pull me in almost immediately, offering the illusion of safety in exchange for loyalty I wasn't ready to give. Somehow, by luck, instinct, or maybe the grace of God, I managed to navigate the politics of the gangs without committing to anyone. It wasn't easy. Every day was a tightrope walk, knowing that one wrong move could leave me standing alone when being alone could prove fatal.

There were no genuine friendships here. Unless you were part of a gang, it was every man for himself. But staying unaffiliated felt like the right move to me. I was a lot of things, but a gang banger wasn't one of them.

I watched the older guys who ran the yard to learn how they survived. They didn't flinch at the sight of blood; they didn't blink at pain. They saw the world as a place where only the strong survived, and the weak were destined to be crushed. The padlock gang, who always had a weapon close by, were a constant reminder of what could happen if you weren't careful. The little whispers and the threats made in dark corners all carried the same message: Don't let anyone see weakness. Don't let anyone think you're soft. If you do, you're done.

My cellmate was an older guy, built like a brick wall, his body covered in tattoos. He didn't talk much but when he did, it was usually to tell me what I was doing wrong. His advice wasn't kind, but it was worth listening to. "Keep your head down," he'd say. "Don't start shit, but don't let them see you're scared. You show weakness here, you'll be someone's bitch in no time." He wasn't wrong.

By the time I'd been in Fort Dodge for six months, I didn't recognize myself anymore. I was barely twenty, and although I'd felt part of myself dying and hardening for years, by the time I was twenty, prison had made me a much harder person.

I'd learned how to take a punch and keep moving, how to look someone in the eye and not back down. The fearlessness that once allowed me to break into houses was nothing compared to the fearlessness that was required to survive in prison. Nothing.

In the midst of the cruel brutality in Fort Dodge, Daisy gave birth to our baby girl, Annie.

I wasn't there to hold Daisy's hand, to see my daughter take her first breath, or to experience the magic of that moment in person. But I did get to talk to Daisy a few minutes after the birth.

The emotions that hit me were indescribable: Joy, regret, love, and an unbearable ache for the life I was missing.

Within a month, Daisy's mom brought Annie to see me at the Fort Dodge prison. Sitting in that sterile visiting room, I held my daughter for the first time. She was so small, so perfect. In that moment, I wanted to be better. I wanted to be the father she deserved.

Daisy and her mom didn't just send letters or wait for me to reach out, they showed up.

Even though the drive was three hours long each way, the gas money was tight, and worries weighed them down, they made the trip. They spent hours in an old car with the heater barely working or the air conditioning gasping in the summer heat, just to sit across from me for an hour. Despite living hand-to-mouth, they scraped together whatever they could to load minutes onto my prison phone account so I could call.

Only a few things ever pierced through the endless gray of my prison days. But Daisy, and even more surprisingly, her mother, did. It would have been easy for them to push me aside like a broken piece of their past, to move on with their lives. They had every reason to do that.

Instead, they made me feel like I still mattered, like I wasn't abandoned by the world I had wrecked.

21

NEW DAD

The day I was released from prison in Fort Dodge was overcast, the kind of day where the sky hangs heavy and colorless, as if the world itself is holding its breath, waiting to see what will happen. I stood outside the prison gates with a plastic bag of state-issued belongings and a thousand pounds of uncertainty.

In Iowa, a fifteen-year sentence is rarely served. Practically, you're going to serve more like seven and a half years, and you can get "good time" for good behavior. I did, and I got out in less than two years.

Kat pulled up in an old sedan that had seen better days, the engine knocking as it idled at the curb. I climbed in.

It had been years since I'd seen her. She wasn't exactly family. Kat had been married to my dad once, a long, messy story that ended with his death. Still, somehow, here she was, the only person willing to take a chance on the broken kid he left behind.

We never spoke directly about our relationship, which wasn't strained exactly, but fragile, built just on our shared history with my father. She looked at me like she was trying to find my dad in my face. I knew what she saw because I could see it too. My dad had been the kind of man people wanted to love, loud and funny, with a magnetic personality. But he was also a man who burned bridges faster than he could build them, whose anger and addictions boiled just beneath the surface, invisible until they exploded and shattered everything.

Maybe Kat took me in because of that connection. I was the last living piece of him she could hold on to. It was probably out of guilt, or gratitude, or some tired sense of duty after I'd helped her legally claim the remainder of his estate. I never asked, and she never told me.

Her place was one of the nicer double-wide trailers in one of those strict, clean parks on the edge of Cedar Rapids. In these parks the grass was kept neatly trimmed, siding was power washed twice a year, and the Neighborhood Watch group was as concerned about appearances as it was about safety. It was humble but it was safe.

Daisy and I moved in with Kat, bringing little in the way of plans and lots in the way of hopes.

One moment, I'm a hardened criminal surviving prison, and the next, I'm a wistful young man who is optimistic about a new future. The pivot was extreme. Just like everything had been in my life.

Daisy and I were dysfunctional kids playing house with a real baby, trying to manage a life we were in no way equipped for.

Daisy was doing her best to navigate motherhood with a grace I didn't recognize at the time, and I – well, I was still too caught up in my own unresolved messes to be the partner or father I needed to be. I wanted things my way. I tried to control everything: Where she went, who she talked to, how she acted, because everything I'd been taught was that control meant security.

But Daisy wasn't built to be controlled any more than I was.

She had a strength about her, a stubbornness that I mistook for defiance when really, it was an asset, a survival skill baked into her the same way it had been baked into me.

There were good times, sure. Fleeting moments when we laughed together, when a future seemed possible, even if it was shaky. And nights when we stayed up too late, talking about dreams we didn't have the resources to pursue. But big, obvious cracks were there from the start, threatening everything we were trying to build together.

Living under Kat's roof didn't make it easier. I didn't see it then, but now I can admit it: I was a terrible houseguest. Ungrateful, rude, disrespectful. I acted like the world owed me something just for surviving it. Kat, for all her patience, had her limits. I thought she was too hard on me, too critical. But looking back, she was just trying to set boundaries. I was quick to rebel against any kind of boundary after the intense confinements of prison, and jail before it, and juvenile detention before that. In her house, where she'd already been challenged too many times, I was a cocktail of problems.

It didn't take long for it all to fall apart. Daisy and I fought more often than we laughed. Kat and I avoided each other as tension between us grew. Eventually, my immaturity and brokenness caused the collapse of our fragile family structure.

It would take a lot of years and a lot more brokenness before I could look back and see things clearly, before I could understand that Kat had offered me a lifeline when she had every reason to walk the other way. And that Daisy had given me more love and forgiveness than I deserved. At the time, though, all I could see was the wreckage behind me and the confusing, uncertain road ahead.

I didn't have a plan that Sunday morning.

I stepped out of Kat's double-wide with fifteen dollars stuffed in the pocket of my thrift-store jeans and an ache inside me that I couldn't name.

I flagged down a cab like I had somewhere important to be, when the truth was, I didn't know what I was chasing or where I'd go. All I knew was that the life I was living, the endless loop of mistakes, regret, loneliness, anger, fear and confusion, was a dead end, and I couldn't stomach another day of it.

The cab ride was short, just a few minutes across town, but I felt like I'd crossed a canyon. The First Assembly of God church appeared ahead of me, imposing in the way anything unknown can feel. As I stepped out of the cab and paid the driver, the fifteen bucks gone just like that, I was struck by a wave of fear. What was I even doing here? I didn't belong in a place like this. I was a screw-up. A thief. A kid who had made nothing but bad choices. But underneath all that noise in my head, a voice said, *"Keep walking."*

Looking back, I know now it was God who planted that thought in me, that whisper telling me that if I was ever going to break free, I couldn't do it alone. I didn't recognize His voice yet, didn't know enough to call it faith.

Inside, the church was a maze of warm hallways that smelled like coffee and floor wax filled with unfamiliar faces. I wandered for a few minutes, feeling painfully out of place, until I somehow found my way to a small office. That's where I met Brad Singleton.

Brad wasn't what I expected. No suit and tie, no forced smile or polished sermon. He was young, with a worn Bible on his desk and the kind of presence that made you want to sit still for a minute. His eyes were sympathetic and understanding; it seemed like they were looking past my exterior and deeper into my soul. It was like he could see all my mess and yet, he didn't flinch.

We talked for a little while that day. I don't even remember what the conversation was about. Probably something simple, something forgettable on the surface. But it wasn't the words that mattered, it was the way he leaned in when I spoke, the way he looked at me like I was worth his time. To him, I wasn't a burden or a problem to be solved. I was just a kid with a shot at something different.

Brad didn't just shake my hand and wish me luck that day. He pursued me.

He asked for my phone number. He'd text me, he'd take me to lunch, he'd ask me how I was doing. He was trying to pastor me.

But my old habits would pull me under again, and when I'd find myself behind bars yet again, he would be the only one who wouldn't write me off. He'd show up. Again and again. Later, he'd be the only one sitting across from me in jail visitation rooms. No matter what happened, Brad talked to me like I had worth. Somehow, he was always able to see the kid he met that first Sunday; still in there somewhere, fighting to get out.

I didn't know it yet, but meeting Brad Singleton would mark the first real crack in the walls I had built around myself.

It was a small fracture where light – God's light – would eventually come pouring in.

22

QUICK STOP

For a while, it almost seemed like I might make it.

I had struggled to find a "normal" life and now I had a job at a gas station just off the main drag in Cedar Rapids. It wasn't glamorous, but it was honest, or at least it started that way. I'd stand behind the counter, counting out change and pretending the hum of the coolers and the "ding" of the door chime were enough to drown out the voice calling to me from somewhere inside my head.

But that old pull, that old hunger, never really left.

It lurked beneath the surface like a cancer in short-lived remission, waiting for the right moment to flare up again. It didn't take long before I was slipping bills from the register into my pocket and cracking beers in the cooler when no one was watching.

After my relationship with Daisy fell apart, I started seeing a girl named Mikayla. In some ways, Mikayla was everything I wasn't. She was steady, responsible, dependable, and a little too good for me. She had a decent job, her own apartment, and a Dale Earnhardt-edition Monte Carlo she kept immaculate. Riding shotgun in her car, I could almost convince myself that I was becoming the man she thought I could be. But the truth was, the low wages I was being paid and the long hours at work only made other options more tempting. Every day at the gas station, I thought about the easy money of a burglary. The idea brewed in the back of my mind, reminding me regularly that the old methods were still doable.

It was about ten months into this fragile new life that I gave in. One night, frustrated and longing for something I couldn't identify, I broke into a house. It wasn't planned like the old days; there was no casing the place, no careful timing. It was reckless and impulsive, a devilish itch that demanded to be scratched. I used Mikayla's Monte Carlo without considering that the rumble of the engine would be far too loud in the quiet neighborhood I was targeting.

Someone outside walking their dog saw me slip in through the side door of a house where I didn't belong. I didn't even have to wait for the sirens to know it was over.

I could feel it in my bones.

Sin rarely kicks the door in.

It slides in quietly, like a note pushed under the door
when no one is looking.

I was the guy behind the counter at the convenience store.
Fresh out of prison. New start. Clean slate, or at least as clean
as I knew how to make it. I had made promises, real ones.
I promised myself. I promised other people. I promised I would
never break into houses again. Never live that life again.
Never go back. And I meant it. With everything in me.

If evil had shown up that day and said, "Go commit a burglary,"
I would have laughed it out of the room. I would have said,
"Get behind me, Satan."

The line in the sand was clear. That door was locked.

But that's not how it works.

Sin starts softer than that. Reasonable, even.

"It is fine to have a beer at work. You're stressed.
You've earned it."

"It's fine to take a pack of gum. You'll pay it back later."

"It's fine to grab a roll of quarters off the safe. No one will notice.
You are not hurting anyone."

Each thought slipped in like it belonged there. None of them
felt like the thing I swore I would never do again. They felt small.
Manageable. Harmless.

That is the danger.

Sin doesn't usually drag you away in chains. It walks beside you,
step by step, shrinking the distance between who you are and
who you swore you would never be, or never be again.

It stretches you just enough that the next step does not feel so far. And then the next. And then the next. What once would have horrified you starts to feel familiar. Justified. Normal.

I am not telling this story to dodge responsibility.
I own every choice I made. Every action was mine.
Full stop. But understanding how sin works matters, because it shows us where to build defenses.

If we only guard the obvious lines, the big dramatic sins, we leave the small cracks wide open. And those cracks are where sin wedges those cracks wide open.

That is why we need guardrails, not just good intentions. It's why we need accountability, people who can see us clearly when we start explaining things away. Why we need to be in the Word daily, letting truth recalibrate our thinking before lies start sounding reasonable. Why confession matters, not because God does not already know, but because secrecy is where sin grows strongest. Why we need the Holy Spirit, not as a distant concept, but as an active guide, and why we need to listen when He nudges, even when the nudge feels inconvenient.

Because sin does not usually announce itself.

It whispers.

And if we are not paying attention, we start answering back.

The goal is not perfection. The goal is awareness. Humility. A life lived in the light, where nothing has room to slide in unnoticed.

That is how freedom is gained and protected.

Not by locking the front door by yourself, believing you're secure, but by having a room full of people who are watching for anything to slip under the door that could later swing it wide open.

23

FLORIDA MAN

Somehow, I managed to get out of there without the cops catching me. When I got back to Mikayla's apartment, panic-stricken and stupid with fear, she leaped into action. Despite everything I'd done, she didn't turn her back on me, didn't yell or ask a hundred questions; she just threw some things into a bag and handed me the keys. We drove through the night to get to Chicago, and from there, I caught a bus headed south.

I barely made it onto the bus as I stuffed a crumpled wad of stolen cash in my pocket. I wasn't thinking clearly, only that my brother was in Florida, and if I could just get there, maybe I could buy myself a little time. Maybe I could make a fresh start there, but if not, at least it would be another place to hide. I told myself I could disappear there, outrun my mistakes.

Deep down, I think I already knew: You can change your scenery, but you can't outrun who you are or what you've done.

The bus rumbled beneath me, the old shocks groaning as they hit every pothole on the Illinois highway. The landscape changed as we traveled south, cornfields giving way to thick forests, forests thinning into wide open stretches of swampy land. I barely slept; I was too wired to relax. Each stop blurred into the next: a gas station, a diner or fast-food joint, bathroom stalls covered in graffiti that told of the rage and despair that I felt.

The ride was long. God, it was long.

When the bus finally rolled into Florida, it was like hitting a wall of wet heat. Palm trees lined the sidewalks, their fronds bending under the weight of the humidity. I stepped off the bus and didn't even get a full breath in before they were on me.

Two officers. No words. No hesitation.

I didn't fight. What was the point? Their boots struck the hot pavement with a steady, menacing rhythm, matching the pounding in my head as they marched me to a waiting cruiser. They shoved me inside, and I stared out at a city that didn't know I existed.

Forty-five days. That's how long I spent sitting in the Pasco County Jail, watching the mold crawl up the corners of the walls and listening to the fluorescent lights buzz like a swarm of angry bees. I had run, but you can't outrun yourself. You can't outrun the choices that stain your soul.

The day the extradition orders came through, it wasn't a surprise, it was an inevitable sentence. They shackled my wrists and ankles so tightly the blood in my veins throbbed against the metal. They didn't even pretend to be gentle as they threw me into the back of the transport van. The Florida sun beat down mercilessly, turning the inside of the van into an oven. The guards didn't care. They were just doing a thankless job, moving broken human cargo from one damned place to another.

I thought they'd fly me back to Iowa. A plane, maybe a quick trip. But no. Extradition wasn't a sprint, it was a slow, grinding crawl across the underbelly of America. County by county. Jail by jail.

Like a lot of places I had been, the van smelled like a combination of old sweat, stale cigarettes, and cheap air freshener that did nothing but make the stink worse. Two other inmates sat on the bench seat across from me, their eyes dull and wary. We didn't speak. In the transport world, silence and anonymity were far safer than conversation and familiarity.

They fed us cheap fast food at every other stop – soggy burgers, cold fries, soda – and they handed out tiny bottles of water like they were rationing life itself. They tossed plastic jugs into the back for when nature inevitably called. There was no dignity or privacy in that experience, just absolute humiliation.

They gave us cigarettes sparingly, to keep us docile. I hoarded mine like a miser hoards gold since I knew they'd be worth something when I got back to Iowa. I didn't smoke and never have, but survival in this situation wasn't just about drawing another breath, it was about staying two steps ahead of the game, even if you were shackled to the floor of a moving cage.

Somewhere in Georgia, things went sideways.

We were crammed into a dank, dingy holding cell, where the air was so damp you could taste the mildew. An officer stood just close enough, his keys swinging in an absent-minded rhythm at his hip.

Plunged back into the criminal justice system, any humanity I'd regained during my year out in the world evaporated. My darker impulses, just like they had done so many times, took over.

In a flash of foolishness, I lunged for the keys.

I never even touched the key ring before a sharp hiss filled the air.

My face was on fire. Pepper spray. The burning was immediate and absolute. Eyes clamped shut, skin screaming. I hit the floor hard, coughing and gagging, every nerve was an inferno of agony.

Hard hands dragged me backward and slammed the cuffs tighter. The lesson was clear: There would be no escape, and even trying came with consequences.

After that, the details of the trip blurred even more. More jails, more faces, more smells. Each cell looked the same: gray, cold, anonymous. Names didn't matter. Time didn't matter. We were just bodies moving through a system made to contain society's problems, ghosts haunting places no one wanted to be.

When we finally arrived in Iowa, it didn't feel like a homecoming. It felt like walking back into a cage you thought you'd outgrown.

The intake facility loomed ahead, its harsh lights and sharp angles. Concrete and steel. No forgiveness. The van slowed and pulled into the lot, and the guards moved us out like cattle. My legs were stiff and my wrists were numb, but I forced myself forward. Inside, the air was as I remembered it.

But this time, I wasn't a terrified kid seeing this for the first time.

This time, I was the one for whom this was familiar.

"Welcome home," a guard muttered as he unhooked my cuffs.

24

STONE CITY PEN

I t wasn't my first time, but this time was different.

When the bus pulled up to the gates of the Anamosa State Penitentiary, a hush fell over the handful of inmates slouched in their seats. The bravado and nervous cockiness that usually prevailed on every ride into lockup evaporated. Even the seasoned ones, the guys who had worn out their state-issued shoes more than once, sat rigid and silent, eyes fixed straight ahead like soldiers arriving at the front lines.

The prison towered over the neighborhoods around it, looking like something from medieval times.

Anamosa Prison is an enormous stone fortress built in the 1870s from huge blocks of Iowa limestone. It looks more like a medieval castle than a prison, a relic from a time when brutality wasn't a flaw of the system, it was the system. If it weren't for the barbed wire curling like thorny vines across the tops of the walls, it might've been beautiful.

Set right in the middle of the town I'd lived in during my short time with my dad, the town Daisy came from, being assigned here was a strange juxtaposition for me.

139

The door of the bus groaned open, heat and dust spilled in. We stepped out single-file, chains rattling between our ankles, the clink and drag of cuffs as the soundtrack to the hell in front of us.

The CO's, correctional officers, stood at attention, mirrored sunglasses hiding whatever showed in their eyes. Here, there were no shouted insults or threats. They didn't need to bark to keep you in line. The place itself did the talking.

By this time I'd done a lot of time. Clarinda Academy, various city jails, county jails, all the extradition pit-stops, the intake facility, prison at Fort Dodge, all medium-security but nothing prepared me for this. Anamosa wasn't about rehabilitation, time served, or anything of that sort. It was about survival at an even higher level than I'd ever experienced.

Inside the gates, the yard opened up in stark contrast to the walls enclosing it. A cracked basketball court and a few iron workout stations were separated by patches of dead grass. Everything was tired and faded.

The inmates here moved differently too. There was a constant tension in the air, so every motion was calculated and deliberate. In medium-security, disrespect would earn you a black eye or a brutal beating that left you on the ground bleeding. If it went too far, maybe you'd get a few days in solitary confinement.

Here, disrespect would get you killed.

Consequently, the atmosphere was polite in an odd way, with a grim, coded civility. Eye contact was measured. Words were chosen carefully, almost kindly. You didn't bump into someone without apologizing. You didn't borrow something without asking twice. You didn't make a joke at someone's expense unless you knew exactly how far you could push.

The stakes weren't about ego like in Fort Dodge, they were about keeping your teeth.

My cellblock was a dark corridor lined with ancient iron-barred cells. Unlike newer facilities with their electric doors that opened with an electronic buzz and click, with clean metallic lines, this place was ancient. The iron bars were scarred by decades of damage where bodies had rammed into them, or desperate hands had beaten on them. Mechanical levers opened the cells with a metallic groan and the clang of iron on iron. My new home was barely wide enough for a bunk and a stainless steel sink bolted off kilter onto the wall. The window was just a slit maybe four inches by twelve inches, carved high in the stone, letting in a ribbon of light so thin it might as well have been imaginary.

That first night as I laid down on the bare mattress, I stared up at the ceiling covered in stains from old leaks. Listening. Smelling. Feeling. Every sense was alert, tuned to the rhythms of a place where a sound could mean anything. The creak of a door, a whispered name, a hurried footstep…every noise carried a message.

There was no space here for the kind of petty bravado that prevailed in medium-security prisons. There were no kids trying to make a name for themselves. Everyone had already earned their place, and they had earned it with blood.

And yet, despite the ever-present threat that hung like a heavy curtain over every conversation or glance, there was an odd sort of honor here. You didn't start problems if you didn't want problems. You didn't say something if you couldn't back it up. Your word mattered.

The worst thing you could be here wasn't weak – it was fake.

I spent my first weeks walking a tightrope. Watching. Learning. Finding out who ran the block, who controlled the yard, who you could nod to and who you needed to cross the street to avoid. It was exhausting, being that vigilant. Like holding your breath all day while pretending you were breathing just fine.

I understood then why they built Anamosa to look like a castle.

And it did. Built from the same yellow limestone that I'd climbed that day when I'd skipped school, when I was on that cliff where the sheriff called me down, when he'd put me in his car, when he'd taken me to the graveyard. Was that very cliff that I'd climbed that day been where they'd carved the blocks that built this prison? It could have been.

The ancient blocks stacked to make this castle were meant to be escape-proof.

But they were also meant to hold you hostage inside yourself.

My cellmate was a guy affectionately known as Grasshopper. Grasshopper didn't say much in those early days, but he didn't need to. His silence was a warning. He was like a wasp nest that you didn't dare poke. He'd do sets of fifty pushups without breaking a sweat, his knotted arms folding and unfolding like a machine. Every once in a while, he'd glance my way, not with hostility, but with that calculating look seasoned men in prison have, weighing whether you were a problem or a pawn. I knew better than to force conversation. Respect in a place like Anamosa was built through consistently keeping your mouth shut, your eyes open, and your body ready.

The weight pile became my proving ground. Out in the yard, under the wide Iowa sky where the old yellow limestone walls formed a courtyard, we trained. The iron was rusted and rough and the benches were crooked and pitted from years of hard use, but nobody cared. We weren't really training for fitness; we were training to survive being in there with one another. The cinder block of a man who first challenged me, his name turned out to be Rico, watched without a word as I strained under weights I had no business lifting. My hands trembled. My lungs burned. But I didn't quit. That kind of grittiness mattered more than how much weight you could lift. Quitting was weakness, and weakness in a place like this was a scent that drew predators.

Weeks stretched into months, and with every rep, every set where I thought my chest would tear open, something hardened inside me. I grew not just in muscle but in presence. It's a strange thing, how your posture changes when your body strengthens, you stand a little taller, move a little more deliberately. You learn to control your breathing, your face, your emotions. In a place like Anamosa, that control was your armor. It didn't guarantee safety, but it was one more layer between you and the wolves.

Grasshopper finally spoke to me one afternoon, after I dropped a bar back into the rack, my arms shaking from a brutal set. "You ain't soft," he said, nodding once, almost to himself. Coming from him, it was a kind of acceptance. Not friendship, there was no such thing in here, but an acknowledgment that I belonged, at least for now. In a world ruled by silent codes and unforgiving eyes, that was worth more than gold.

The weight pile became more than a place to get stronger. It was church. It was therapy. It was war. Every plate I added to the bar was another piece of the old me stripped away, the reckless boy who had thought he could outrun his demons – gone. Here, under the watchful eyes of killers and lifers, I was forging something new, even if I didn't fully understand it.

Then came books.

In a place that prioritized sharpening your instincts and your punches, it almost felt foolish to chase after something as fragile as words. But I was hungry, starving even, not just for food or respect, but for answers to questions I didn't even have the language for yet. I had spent most of my life reacting, fighting, and clawing my way out of my broken messes, but somewhere deep inside, a small part of me knew that if I didn't find a new way to think, to *be*, I wasn't going to make it.

The prison library smelled like old paper, and it wasn't much to look at. A few battered metal shelves sagged under the weight of torn paperbacks and out-of-date encyclopedias. But it was quiet, a different kind of quiet than the cellblocks, a quiet that didn't feel dangerous. I found the self-help section wedged between True Crime and Westerns. It was a sad little row of books nobody seemed to notice. Faded spines promised things like *How to Rebuild Your Life* and *Change Your Thinking, Change Your Life.* I didn't know if I believed that was possible, but it was enough to get me to crack one open.

Reading was like lifting in those early days: clumsy, painful, and slow. My eyes would skip across sentences, my mind drifting back to fights in the yard, to the weight plates clanging, to the endless loop of bad decisions that had landed me here. But every time I wrestled my way through a paragraph, a strange thing happened. A sentence would grab me by the collar and not let go. It would punch a hole through the fog in my brain and whisper: *"You don't have to stay like this, Kyle."*

I started spending my sixteen cents an hour (the wages I earned wiping down tables and pushing mop buckets) on mailing costs for ordering more books through the prison programs. Some guys laughed at me; some looked at me like I was soft. But I didn't care. I was working on something more important than a reputation. I was fighting for my mind the same way I fought for my turn on the bench press.

And then there was the Bible.

There wasn't a moment of lightning and thunder; it was quiet, almost forgettable. A simple beat-up King James Bible was sitting crookedly on a shelf, like it had been pushed aside repeatedly in favor of something else. I wasn't ready for it, not yet. But the thought of it lingered in my mind, like a seed dropped into dry ground, waiting for rain. I went back to the other books, devouring anything about discipline, resilience, or rebuilding your life from the ashes. There were several that genuinely inspired me to change, taught me the beginnings of the mechanics of change, and gave me tools to survive mentally in a place designed to break you.

But looking back, I can see it as clear as day: Those books were only the beginning. The Bible, that forgotten, dusty thing, was the foundation waiting to be discovered underneath all those other books. I just hadn't dug deep enough to find it yet. It would be years before I felt strong enough to lift that particular weight. But something in me was starting to shift. For the first time, I realized real strength wasn't about the steel you threw around in the yard. There was more.

25

OUT FOR NOW

The air smelled different on the outside of the penitentiary. Crisper somehow, with a kind of promise I didn't know if I could trust. Potential. I stood just beyond the prison gates with a cheap duffel bag slung over my shoulder, feeling smaller than I ever had behind the walls. The weight of the bag was nothing compared to the years of past experiences pressing down on me. I shifted from foot to foot, scanning the lot until I saw him: Brad Singleton.

Same easy smile. Same kind eyes.

Same old minivan rattling as he pulled up to the curb.

He got out and clapped a hand on my back without a second's hesitation, like there hadn't been years and failures and mistakes between us.

"Let's get you home," he said simply.

Home.

That word caught in my chest, unexpected and unwelcome. I didn't have a home.

The drive back to Cedar Rapids from Anamosa felt surreal. Fields blurred as we passed them and the sun slowly set.

I gazed out the window and half-listened as Brad talked about his wife Dianne, his kids, his church, his weightlifting meets … his life. It was the kind of life that once felt as far away as the stars to me, but I was stepping into it.

Brad and Dianne's house was a modest ranch with a small front yard and a garage used as a gym. It wasn't much by the world's standards, but to me, it was like another planet. Inside, it smelled like cinnamon and fresh laundry. Pictures lined the walls: smiling kids, holiday gatherings, messy birthdays. All evidence of life as a real family.

Brad and Dianne had three kids: two daughters and a son. The girls were still in elementary school, full of energy and wild imagination. Their son was just entering middle school, lanky and very bright. They welcomed me and made me feel at home, like I was a fixture in the house, not some ex-con with too much baggage to fit through the door.

The first night, Brad and I tackled the project of drywalling the room that would be mine. It was an unfinished corner of the basement they had set aside. Neither of us had a clue what we were doing. Screws tore through the paper like it was wet tissue, and drywall mud dripped in clumps down the seams. We laughed so hard we cried, and when we finally staggered upstairs, exhausted and covered in dust and mud, it didn't matter that it looked like a disaster zone downstairs. We had done it. It was a beginning.

Every morning after that, Brad and I would meet out in his garage, a shrine to powerlifting, stacked with iron plates and creaky old benches. My years of lifting weights in the prison yard had made me strong, but now I had someone who actually knew how to lift, who could push me and teach me. Brad talked life with me between sets, like it was the most normal thing in the world. Those mornings in the garage turned out to be some of the most healing moments of my life.

Despite a fresh start and all that goodness and support from Brad and his family, there was still a fracture deep inside me. I called myself a Christian at that time and I had even started to believe it some days, but surrender was something else. I hadn't "unclenched my fists" yet to let go of the parts of me that still craved risk and were addicted to self-destruction. In the quiet moments I had to myself, the undertow of old instincts and bad habits was still pulling at my ankles, and my actual turn to Christ would come much later.

During that time at Brad's, I also got to spend more time with my daughter, Annie, who by now was five or six. I'd seen her and she'd seen me a few times when I was in prison.

Daisy, to her credit, allowed me to have her most weekends. She would drop Annie off at Brad's house with a tiny pink backpack bouncing on her shoulders and a guarded smile stretched across her face. Annie's short legs would swing above the floor when she sat on a chair. She had a soft, cautious voice that was so sweet it hurt to hear her laugh, like something delicate I didn't deserve to experience.

Brad, ever patient, would demonstrate for me how to gently engage Annie. He suggested board games, books, little craft projects. I tried. God, I tried. But it was clumsy and forced, like trying to speak a language I had never been taught. I would sit cross-legged on the living room floor, awkwardly holding out a doll or a storybook, while Annie watched me with her wide, solemn eyes. She never fully let her guard down.

Looking back, I think some part of her already understood who and what I was. Even at her young age, she could sense the fault lines in me. Some instincts, especially in kids, are too honest to ignore. Unfortunately, I would prove her right.

I fell in love with the bar scene long before I ever realized it had swallowed me whole. It wasn't the alcohol that drew me in at first, it was the atmosphere, the camaraderie, the bursts of laughter, the sense of belonging. I was a kid with an orphan's heart, and I was desperate for a place to call home. In the dim light and smoky haze of the bar, surrounded by strangers whose smiles didn't come with strings attached, I found a family of the broken, the reckless, and the wandering. People like me.

The Water Cooler became a sanctuary for me where nobody asked hard questions. No one cared where you came from, only that you could hold your liquor and keep the mood alive. The regulars told the same worn-out jokes and sang the same sad songs week after week. I fit right in. We were a congregation of orphaned spirits, each of us half-drowning in our own way, clinging to one another for support. I wasn't an outsider there; I was another voice raised in a drunken chorus.

For a while, the bar scene felt like love, the kind of desperate love you cling to when you've never known anything better. And like all desperate loves, it demanded a price. I didn't notice it at first, but the longer I stayed, the higher the price went. Nights blurred into mornings, and the friendships we forged over shots and cigarettes proved to be as fragile as the promises we made each other at the same time. Still, even knowing that, part of me didn't want to leave. The bar didn't judge me. It welcomed me in my loneliness and gave me a place to belong. And for a heart that had never learned what a real home felt like, what love was, I didn't know that this wasn't it.

And let's be honest. None of this was romantic. It was sad. I was still an undiagnosed bipolar runaway raised in prison. Housed but not healed. I still dealt with manic thoughts. I was self-medicating.

So I didn't mean for it to happen, but who would be surprised that it did? I had moved out from Brad's, moved in with a girl, then in with some other people, I was just bobbing around.

All the cracks in my soul that I had refused to deal with widened. My old habits, including my old thirst for risk and chaos, flooded me like a broken pipe in a dirty basement. It started with a drink. Then another. Then … I broke into another house, just like that. Like I hadn't learned one single thing in all my time being incarcerated.

Like the love that Brad had shown me, letting me move in with his family, wasn't the answer.

So when the cuffs snapped sharply around my wrists again, the only thing more humiliating than the shame I felt was the memory of Annie's guarded little smile, the way she had never leaned all the way into me, fully trusting me. Somewhere deep down, she had known. And she had protected herself.

I wasn't the victim; I had done this to myself, but not just to someone else, to my daughter, to her mother.

I had made a mess again; I destroyed the freedom and stability I'd been given.

Over the next few years, I watched from a distance as Daisy's new boyfriends would fill the role a father was supposed to for Annie, and the space I once occupied in her life shrank. The pain of watching that happen was unbearable, but I felt powerless to change it.

26

WASH, RINSE, REPEAT

By the time I landed my sixth trip to prison, I'd lost any hope that this would be my last stint behind bars. I wasn't angry anymore, not in the aggressive way I had been. I was just tired. Numb. Life had shrunk down to something small and gray, measured in concrete blocks and half-hearted conversations. I wasn't chasing redemption or even survival at that point. I was existing, floating through sad, pointless, empty days. My world was predictable: counted out in chow lines, yard time, and the hollow clank of cell doors locking for the night.

It's also important here to remind you, if your head is spinning a little, that I've simplified an even more complicated story.

If you're thinking, "Wait, how old is he by now? How many times has he been in and out of prison?" The truth is that to streamline all of this, I've blended some things together. It's worth saying for a few reasons – one is so that you won't be confused.

But here's the other: What you should understand is that from my time in placements as a young teenager through my various times in and out of jail, there was no consistency, no stability, no permanence. If there was anything that looked like permanence, it was permanent instability. And that's how it is for kids who move through the system and then into cycles of incarceration. Constant impermanence. Foster placements that might only last a few weeks. Jail that might only last a few days. Staying on someone's couch for a week or two. A court sentence of nine months that's reduced to fewer. To include all of that would be impossible, and it's unnecessary. But what's important for you to understand is what I said first: By the time I landed my sixth trip to prison, I'd lost any hope that this would be my last stint behind bars.

I didn't go to church in jail to find God. I went there to sell drugs.

On this particular day, I had to get some pills to a guy in B block, and chapel was the safest way to do it. I don't remember the sermon. I don't remember the pastor's name.
What I do remember is the janitor.

She was always there, a quiet woman in her late forties, maybe older, maybe younger (jail ages people in strange ways). She wore a faded uniform and kept her eyes down.

That day, as I passed off the pills, a small, sleight-of-hand gesture perfected by survival, there was a sound. A sudden crack of wood against tile. The mop handle had fallen.

It startled all of us. Even the guards looked up.

Then she did something no one expected. She stepped forward. With wrinkled hands and a slight tremble in her voice, she asked the pastor if she could say a few words.
But really, she didn't ask. She just spoke.

She said she'd been mopping the floors of Linn County Jail for eight years. That every night, as the halls emptied and the noise died down, she filled her mop bucket with warm water, a splash of disinfectant... and anointing oil.

She said she prayed over each cell as she worked.
Every corner. Every door. Every bunk. Every soul.

We didn't move. We didn't breathe.

"I know y'all don't see me," she said, "but I see you. And more importantly, God sees you."

I don't know the theology of anointing oil.
But I know what it feels like when someone speaks life over you with fire in their eyes and tenderness in their voice.

She looked out over the chapel and said, "You think no one's fighting for you? I been fighting for you on my knees for eight years. You think no one cares? I care. God cares. And this mop water's got more of heaven in it than you'll ever know."

I felt my heart catch in my throat.
I felt something deeper than fear or shame. I felt seen.

She said it softly, but with so much force it cracked
the room open:

"God loves you. Not the future you. Not the cleaned-up you.
He loves you now. Right now. Exactly as you are."

I'd heard those words before. But never like that.
She wasn't preaching. She was pouring.
And we were the ground catching her rain.

And I broke.

Right there, in the middle of the most corrupt thing I'd done that week, I bawled like a kid. So did the guy next to me.
So did the dealer from C block and the lifer from A.
It was like time stopped, and the Spirit of God swept through those cinderblock walls with the fragrance of Pine-Sol.

Then she picked up her mop and walked out.

The pastor never reclaimed the mic.

That was fifteen years ago. And once I told this story,
God showed up again.

Within four hours of publishing this story the first time,
I reconnected with her.

We filmed part of Killing Kyle Orth together.

Now, she's part of this same thing we all are – this project
to use my story, and the story so many of us share – so that
others might find freedom.

Because it's all of us: that janitor, a woman without a title,
without a stage, she delivered a sermon
that still gets me choked up.

She didn't come to save us. She came to serve. And in doing so,
she became the loudest gospel I'd ever heard.

That opportunity is waiting for each of us, every day.
I'm here for it. How 'bout you?

The latest joint that I was locked up in was different from the other places I'd been tossed into. It didn't have the wild, pent-up aggression of Anamosa or the desperate energy of the medium security joints. It was quieter here, in a way that was almost eerie. Men shuffled through routines like they were sleepwalking, their dreams and hopes long gone. I blended right in, another jaded face in a sea of them. Bettering myself wasn't even on my radar. That was a young man's game, and I felt a thousand years old.

Then one day a strange rumor traveled through the prison. Grinnell College was offering a liberal arts program inside the prison. At first, I thought it was a joke, a cruel trick the system was playing on us to stir false hope.

But the more I heard, the more intriguing the rumor became. There were going to be a handful of openings for students, and actual college professors teaching real classes for real credits. The idea came like a thin ray of sunlight in a boarded-up house. I didn't dare get my hopes up too high – not yet – but I did hope it was true.

I still remember the day I first saw the poster on the prison wall, its edges curled like a treasure map. I was in my early twenties by then: lost, stumbling through a life that was totally off course. I couldn't read very well, and when I spoke, my words got jumbled and awkward, and my writing skills were at the elementary level. But I had a GED and a strong desire to be more than the sum of my mistakes.

In the controlled environment of a correctional facility, college programs had once offered a glimmer of hope for prisoners, a promise of transformation and a future. But by the time I'd arrived, those programs had all but disappeared, gutted from budgets during the harsh reforms of the '90s. Yet here, against all odds, was another chance: a program put together by Grinnell College. It was a name that, at the time, meant nothing to me. I had no idea that Grinnell was one of the nation's most prestigious liberal arts colleges, a place that produced judges and authors and researchers. *Where I came from* produced convicts with rap sheets thicker than textbooks.

I applied on a dare to my own despair. I fumbled my way through an application process I barely understood. I needed a way out, a chance to learn how to think, how to see the world that existed beyond the bars and the walls in my mind that confined me.

27

COLLEGE BOY

Grinnell's program for prison inmates was controversial. Critics argued that, instead of offering practical trades, it wasted time on liberal arts, a discipline they deemed impractical for inmates.

But the liberal arts were exactly what I needed.

And I got in.

In the quiet hours of evening classes, with soft discussions filling a room that felt like a refuge, I began to see the power of a well-taught concept.

I learned to question the obvious, to analyze the world with a newfound clarity that transcended the limitations of my past. Every text we read, every debate we engaged in, chipped away at the chains that had bound my thinking for so long. It wasn't just about learning history or philosophy, it was about learning to reason, to challenge the narratives that had defined me, and to imagine a future where I could be more than a mugshot.

Emily was our instructor. She didn't belong in a place like this. She stood out. She was so much light in a dark place. The visiting room wasn't built for someone like her, a fresh-faced graduate from Grinnell who had no business inside these walls except for the wall she was determined to break down.

She was waiting, sitting stiff-backed in a metal chair, in the visiting room, with her hands folded neatly in her lap and a leather-bound notebook resting on the table. Around us, COs (corrections officers) stood posted at the door, their eyes darting among us like they were waiting for something to go wrong. Inmates shuffled past, some dragging their feet, others with their heads down. Conversations buzzed in the background, but her eyes were steady, focused on something beyond the present, already envisioning what this place could become.

From the first day of class, Emily stood at the front of the room, her notebook open, a piece of chalk in her hand. She looked at us. She didn't look through us, or past us, but at us. Like we were students, not inmates. Like we belonged in class, not just in prison.

The lessons weren't always easy. I struggled with the language, with the abstract ideas that seemed to dance just out of reach. Gradually, despite my missteps and doubts, I began to understand that the beauty of the liberal arts lay in its imperfection. It was in the messy process of learning, of questioning and sometimes failing, that I discovered a resilience I never knew I possessed.

In that unlikely classroom, the transformative power of education took root. It wasn't about acquiring a job or learning a trade; it was about awakening a sense of self-worth, about realizing that every person, no matter how lost or broken, carried the potential for growth. With every class, I learned not just to read and write but to think critically, to challenge assumptions, and to reclaim a piece of my identity that had long been suppressed.

One of the most unexpected turns in my time in the program came in the form of Professor Lingrum. He was a world-renowned expert on the reptile brain, but instead of lecturing us on cold-blooded creatures, he taught a neurology course that forced us to examine ourselves not just as humans, but as animals.

The first time he walked into the classroom, I could tell he was different. Some of the other professors seemed overly cautious, as if they were afraid of saying something wrong. Professor Lingrum was confident but not arrogant, and his voice was calm and direct. He had the look of someone who had spent a great deal of time thinking about things that most people ignored.

He started the first class with a question: "What makes you think you're different from any other animal?"

Silence.

A few guys shifted in their seats, exchanging glances, waiting for someone else to speak first. Then, Professor Lingrum leaned against the desk, arms crossed and continued. "You might believe it's intelligence, self-awareness, morality... but strip all that away, and you're still just a creature trying to survive."

That set the tone for everything that followed. The class wasn't about memorizing brain structures or regurgitating facts. It was about understanding ourselves at the most fundamental level. We dissected the way our brains functioned; how instinct, impulse, and emotion dictated more than we realized.

One lesson in particular hit me hard. We were studying attention, focus, and the way different brains process information. ADHD – attention deficit hyperactivity disorder – came up, and I braced myself for the usual narrative. The disorder, the deficit, the problem to be fixed. But Lingrum didn't see it that way.

"What if I told you ADHD isn't a disorder?" he asked, scanning the room. "What if it's an advantage?"

That got my attention. I had spent years feeling like my brain worked against me, like I was wired wrong. School had always been a struggle, not because I wasn't smart but because I couldn't sit still and focus the way they wanted me to. Trying to sit and focus felt to me like trying to run in deep mud and I always fell short.

But Lingrum explained it differently. He talked about how ADHD brains were built for high-stimulus environments, how they thrived in chaos, how they were made for quick thinking and adaptability. "You're not broken," he said. "Your brain just isn't designed for the box society wants to put you in."

That was a lightbulb moment for me, a revelation. I had always thought of my restlessness, my need for movement, my tendency to hyperfocus on things that interested me as weaknesses. But what if they weren't? What if they were strengths I had never learned to harness?

That class did more than teach me about neurology. It made me see myself differently. It gave me permission to stop trying to fit into a mold that was never meant for me. And for the first time, I started to wonder: What else had I been getting wrong about myself?

That program, with all its controversies and imperfections, offered a cornerstone of a new life that I could build. It provided a bridge for me from the darkness of confinement to a life illuminated by knowledge and possibility. Grinnell, with its storied legacy and commitment to the liberal arts, unknowingly handed me some of the most powerful tools I could ever acquire. And though I entered as a depressed and destitute inmate, I emerged, slowly and surely, with a vision of a brighter future that was truly my own.

Looking back now, I see that those days in the classroom were not just about earning a few academic credits. They were about learning to see the world differently, to understand that the power of thought and reason could be the most potent means of liberation.

When you're homeless, you don't wake up, you come to.
You're never rested, you just survived the night.

You shift on the cold concrete stairwell that kept you
a little bit hidden, brushing away last night's rainwater with
the sleeve of a hoodie that smells like shame.

Sometimes shame smells like mildew.

My hoodie did.

You wake up with an aching back, your teeth throb,
and your stomach reminds you it's empty before you even
remember where you are.

And still, the world moves. The sun rises. Cars hiss by.
People walk fast with coffee in hand and phones pressed to
their ears. No one makes eye contact. They glance, then look
through you, like you're a ghost they don't want to believe in.

It's a strange thing to be alive and yet completely invisible.

You hear people say, "Why don't they just get a job?"
As if it were that simple. As if you weren't dragging a
mountain behind you.

Well, more like a valley. A canyon.

Try applying for a job when you haven't showered in a week,
when you don't own a phone, when your ID was stolen or lost
two cities ago. Try showing up to an interview when the only
shoes you have are duct-taped together, and your face
is swollen from sleeping upright in the cold.

And even if you do get the job, your wages are garnished before
you see a dollar. Your probation officer demands check-ins, but
you don't have a ride. And addiction? It's not a choice. It's a false
friend that has you chained up. It's in control – not you.

Mental illness follows close behind, nipping at your ears, whispering lies so loud they drown out any positive thoughts.

You want to change. You just don't know how.

And you live with this heavy ache that maybe you are too far gone, too broken, too dirty to ever be free of this.

But I need you to know something.

If you're in that place – if you're somehow seeing this curled up behind a dumpster or riding a bus just to stay warm – I see you.

I've been there. Really there.

Not crashing on a couch or living out of a car,
I mean eating out of garbage cans and counting steps between public restrooms. I mean pacing all night under streetlamps because it's not safe to sleep.

You are not worthless. You are not beyond redemption.
You are not invisible to the One who sees all.

There is hope.

There is healing.

There is Jesus.

But chances are, if you're reading this,
you're not in that spot.

Listen: I didn't fix myself. I didn't climb out with willpower or hustle. A man can't pull himself up by his bootstraps when he doesn't have boots.

No – God came for me. He sat with me in my brokenness before I ever lifted my head. He loved me when I couldn't look at myself. And that same love – that same healing – is available to you, and maybe through you.

So if you're reading this and you walk the sidewalks of life with comfort and routine: slow down. That person you stepped over is someone's son. Someone's daughter. Someone made in the image of God. Maybe you can't fix everything. But a smile? A prayer? A moment of dignity? Maybe more?

A lot of people sacrificed way past the point of what was comfortable in order for me to be where I am now.

Not because they loved me so much but because they loved God so much.

And that happened because God loved them so much first – and then His love made its way through them to me.

God loves you too.

28

WINTER AND HOPE

When my release came from prison, it was in the dead of winter.

The transport guard opened the door of the prison van in downtown Cedar Rapids, it was winter, freezing cold, and I was homeless.

For two or three weeks I survived on the brutally cold winter streets of a Midwestern city in January. So I was physically exhausted and mentally defeated when I walked through the doors of the homeless shelter. Mission of Hope.

College in prison gave me newfound problem-solving skills, but not the kind of specific training that would be immediately practical, but somehow, those critical thinking skills had helped me not turn right back to crime.

Instead of finding my way back into trouble, I found the shelter.

It was at full capacity so they put my name on a waiting list; it was another week before I could get a bed. When they finally let me in, I'd been thrown yet another lifeline, but the realities of shelter life were far from comfortable.

There are places in every city where hope is more than a word, the thin line between despair and something holy tips toward redemption.

That's what Mission of Hope was meant to be. Not just a shelter, not just a nonprofit, but a gateway for souls teetering at the edge.

The Mission of Hope ministry was born in the heart of a woman who had no use for titles or praise. Her name was spoken in reverent tones by those who knew her, but she was far from famous: Barb Furman.

But to those of us on the streets, once each of us learned who she was, she became a legend, a warrior draped in prayer and street grit, fearless in her love and ferocious in her obedience to God. You could find her on her knees in a urine-splattered alleyway, hands pressed to the back of some trembling addict, whispering the name of Jesus between sobs and spiritual fire. She wandered through trap houses and tent cities like an angel sent straight from the throne room of heaven. She didn't flinch at the sight of the crack pipe in someone's hand. She saw what most people were too clean, too scared, or too proud to see: image-bearers of God buried beneath society's rubble. From that place of raw obedience, Mission of Hope was born.

At its best, Mission of Hope wasn't a program, it was a movement, a living expression of the gospel of Jesus Christ. People didn't just get a meal; they got seen. They didn't just find shelter; they found dignity. She laid the foundation with nothing but faith, a few sandwiches, and the kind of love that costs you everything. But over time, as with many movements, the flames of the fire began to go out.

I arrived years later, long after she had handed off the reins to others. The shelter was still operating but something was missing. The mission had become a machine. Still a well-intentioned one, but there's nothing like a founder's fire.

It was being run by three women, and though I know they meant well, their focus was sharp, but in a different direction. Instead of shepherding souls, they were policing behavior. Instead of grace, there were policies. The meals were hot and the cots were clean, but the atmosphere was more clinical. It wasn't that they were cruel, just disconnected. You could be falling apart inside, but as long as your shoes were tied and your bed was made, you passed inspection, and that team wasn't as good at seeing it as Barb had been.

But God was at work nevertheless. He always is.

It was there that I first heard the name Bart Woods.

Bart wasn't a staff member; he was on the board of directors. But when I was there, broken and searching, God was setting the stage for something bigger. I didn't know it then, but Bart would become one of the most influential people in my life. A mentor. A friend. A man who, like the mission's founder, burned with the fire of genuine faith. After my time at the Mission ended, abruptly and with more shame than closure, Bart stepped in.

He saw what I had seen. The rigid systems. The robotic enforcement of rules. The way it had traded holy ground for red tape. And he did what few have the courage to do: He cleaned house. It wasn't about revenge or ego, it was about revival.

That moment marked the beginning of a long, intentional process to bring Mission of Hope back to its roots. The shelter portion eventually shut down. Some saw that as a death, but it wasn't. It was pruning.

Mission of Hope still stands. No longer as a place with beds and curfews, but as a ministry with its pulse back. It serves meals. It helps with rent. It shows up where people are hurting. Barb's nature, the founder who held crack addicts like sons and kissed the foreheads of the forgotten, is there once again.

But … I get ahead of myself.

Days into my time as a resident there, at the encouragement of the staff, I began attending their Bible studies. I wasn't particularly interested in religion, but the meetings offered a chance to sit somewhere quiet. Life in a homeless shelter is better than life on the streets during winter in the Midwest, and it's better than prison, but it's not exactly living the dream.

The staff talked about Jesus as if He was a friend, someone who cared about people like me. It was a strange idea, and while I wasn't ready to embrace it, I couldn't dismiss it entirely either. I had always clung to the belief that a greater force was out there, a mysterious presence watching over us. Yet the notion that Jesus was that divine presence never made sense to me. I found myself endlessly questioning. "Why Jesus? Of all the spirits and ghosts that might haunt the universe, why Him?" It felt silly to pursue theological musings when simply surviving mattered so much more.

Survival had been my relentless battle, a daily war against hunger, hardship, and despair. The luxury of pondering theological matters was frivolity – even though I didn't know that word at the time.

I have always believed in a higher power. But the idea that an omnipotent force would choose to take the form of a man

– one who suffered, died, and rose again – seemed more like a fairy tale than a tangible truth.

In the darkness of my days, a brutal paradox haunted me: If the all-powerful God of the Bible truly reigned over everything, why did endless suffering exist? Every injustice and evil deed that I experienced or witnessed was another brick in the wall between me and believing this could be true. I wondered whether this divine force, God, was ever truly compassionate or merely an eerie spiritual myth crafted to explain an indifferent, ruthless universe. I felt caught between the promise of salvation and the unyielding misery of the world. I knew that my understanding of God was as fractured and tormented as the life I had known. But for the first time in many years, maybe since my time living with Brad Singleton, a tiny seed of interest began to sprout.

In those days, Mission of Hope had a lot of hardened hearts passing through cold hallways, so the spiritual pulse of the place was flickering faintly beneath the surface. But every now and then, you'd catch a glimpse of someone who didn't quite fit the mold. That's where Betty came in.

Her name is Betty Criddle, and back then, I didn't know what to make of her. She was a small granny, but the kind who gets her hair done once a week and who is always put together and proper, and who is out and about around town.

She's also the kind who puts in time at places like Mission of Hope with a weathered Bible clutched close to her chest like a compass in a storm. You'd find her at the mission before sunrise, slowly making her way through the building, whispering prayers into corners, brushing her fingers over the backs of chairs as if anointing them with invisible oil.

I thoughts she was nuts.

Who prays over walls and furniture?

Who cries while praying for people they don't even know?

But Betty did. Every day, and with a passion so raw and sincere it unnerved me. At the time, my heart was still too hardened to recognize the kind of power she was tapping into.

Looking back now, I know what I was witnessing wasn't madness, it was spiritual warfare. Betty was a warrior in a grandma's skin. She believed in me long before I ever gave her a reason to. Every time I fell, she was there, whether in person or through prayer, cheering me on like a one-woman army of faith. To this day, she remains one of my biggest champions. I can still hear her voice in my head sometimes, urging me to keep going, reminding me of who I am in Christ. I might've dismissed her as an eccentric old woman, but something she was doing with her presence and her prayers broke through, and we became friends.

After I'd been at Mission of Hope several weeks, I was offered a job as a third-shift worker. It wasn't much, mostly cleaning and keeping an eye on things during the night, but it came with a small private room. Having a space to myself, no matter how small, was a victory and a step toward rebuilding my life again.

I threw myself into the job, grateful for the opportunity. For the first time since my latest release from prison, I could see that I was making progress. This job was a shot at doing something good, something that might help me find some kind of purpose.

But I wasn't ready, not really. On the surface, I tried to help other men who were struggling, but the weight of my own baggage kept pulling me down. I couldn't separate my own unresolved problems from the problems of the people around me. Their anger, their fear, their shame also festered inside me, painful reminders of the things I still hadn't faced. Though I wanted to make a difference in their lives, I wasn't equipped to do so effectively. I was too broken. Instead of rising to the occasion, I crumbled. Sometimes I'd show up for my shift drunk, just numbing the ache inside. Other times I'd collapse in exhaustion, zoning out on the job, too tired and too hollow to care much about anything.

After a few months of this, as I was sitting in a coffee shop one day, an idea struck me out of nowhere: I should sell cars. It was an absurd thought for so many reasons: I had no experience in sales, no "professional" clothing to look the part, and – most absurd of all – no driver's license! If I couldn't legally drive a car, how did I expect to sell them? But the idea, unlike so many of my ideas, didn't flash away in a minute. It stayed all day. It sounded ridiculous, but I believed selling cars would give me a desperately needed new identity, one where I could rise above the "loser" label that had haunted me for so long.

I had always held "car salesmen" in high esteem. I thought of them like doctors and lawyers. The seed for this idea had been planted when I was just a kid in a foster home. I had met a man who was, in my eyes, the coolest guy in the world: A car salesman who was smooth, charming, and confident. He talked about his work with superlatives…it was a grand adventure, the biggest, the best, the most, the greatest … and

I hung on his every word. If only I could be like him! That perception stuck with me.

When I had been locked up, I had stumbled across a self-help book that promised high earnings through selling, even if you lacked a formal education. Those words stuck with me too.

The morning after my coffee shop revelation, I dug through the donated clothes at the shelter until I found enough pieces to sort of resemble a suit. The jacket was too big, the yellow striped shirt faded and dated, with a huge butterfly collar. The baggy dress pants were too short, the belt much too long, and the tie, well, poorly tied. My scuffed old prison shoes completed the look.

But I walked the two miles to the only car dealership I knew of. My mind whirled with conflicting thoughts all the way. Here I was, trying to reinvent myself with clothes that didn't fit, and also desperately hoping that, somehow, this mismatched ensemble would mask both my visible and invisible shortcomings.

As I stepped inside the dealership the energy shifted; at once I felt both intimidated and exhilarated. The showroom was filled with rows of immaculate cars. Every surface sparkled, and the air carried a crisp scent of new leather. It was a temple of sleek machinery where polished BMWs and Fords gleamed under the lights. These cars were symbols of ambition, status, and success, waiting to be worshiped by their future owners.

I walked in and asked to speak with the manager. The receptionist gave me a skeptical look but called him anyway. He came out, took one look at me, and it was instantly clear that he had decided he didn't want to waste his employees' time on me. He led me into his office.

He was a striking figure, a blend of cool confidence and an undeniable toughness that commanded respect. He had a way about him that was both refined and dangerous, like a modern-day mafia don who had earned his power on the streets. Dressed in a sharply tailored suit, he projected authority to a guy like me.

If you had walked in, what you would have seen is that his office was a cramped, cluttered room that somehow had an air of power, danger and inconvenience.

And you would have seen me in cobbled together clown suit from the clothes closet at a homeless shelter sitting across a large wooden desk from a car dealership sales manager.

You learn things in the streets and in prison, and you get very good at reading people.

I could tell he'd know when someone was bluffing their way through life. I sat across from him, feeling the weight of my own inadequacy: no education, no license, dozens of felonies, even more misdemeanors, no job history, no references … but still, here I was.

Now what?

"Where did you go to high school?" he asked.

"I didn't. I dropped out in sixth grade," I replied.

"Do you have a criminal record?"

"Yes. Fifty-eight felonies and more than a hundred misdemeanors."

"Do you have a driver's license?"

"Nope."

He stared at me, baffled. "Why did you come here? You had to know you'd need a diploma, a clean record, and a license, right?"

I looked him straight in the eye and said, "Because every day you don't hire me, your company is losing money."

He laughed, shook his head, and hired me on the spot.

29

THE SHOWROOM

The world of car dealerships is a beast with a thousand faces.

From the outside, it looks like shiny new paint and polished chrome, a place where dreams are brokered with handshakes and monthly payments. But on the inside? It's a circus. The phones never stop ringing. The deals never stop falling apart and coming back together again like the accordion in a jack-in-the-box. Coffee-fueled mornings blur into adrenaline-pumped evenings, where you're either riding high on a big sale or trying to shake off the funk of a customer who just ghosted you after five test drives. Every day feels like a poker game with confusing rules like bluff, charm, and push until someone folds. And if you're not wired for it, it'll chew you up and spit you out without blinking.

There's a grime beneath the glossy cars that's not much of a secret, a kind of tolerated sleaze that lives in the margins. The industry has an uncanny ability to take nobodies, jack-offs with no discipline or direction, and hand them a path to a six-figure lifestyle just for learning how to finesse people the right way. It's a magnet for egos, a breeding ground for broken moral compasses, and yet, oddly, also a haven for comeback stories. People reinvent and rebrand themselves here. Some dealers lie like that's actually their job; others sell like they're saving lives. And the line between the two is fuzzy and moving. It's not for the faint-hearted or the soft-spoken; it's a grind that demands sharp instincts, a stomach for pressure, and a mouth that can sell rain to a thundercloud.

During my first weeks at the dealership I felt like I had been dropped into a different universe. I had entered this world with determination to learn, to adapt, and to prove that I could be more than the sum of the events in my troubled past, but I truly didn't know what I was doing. I was a novice in the world of high-end car sales, fumbling through sales processes, trying to decode the art of persuasion, and listening intently to more experienced colleagues as they worked their magic with every customer. There was a beauty in watching them take a "no" and turn it into a resounding "yes," and that transformation symbolized a power I'd long been denied in every other aspect of my life.

Every day was a lesson. I spent long hours shadowing my coworkers, absorbing every nuance of their interactions with customers. I watched closely to see how they listened, how they read the room, and how they knew exactly when to push a little harder or step back a bit. I learned that sales wasn't just about the product; it was about reading people, understanding their needs, and building trust. I was determined to master the process of turning hesitation into enthusiasm, fear or doubt into excitement. That ability to convert "no" into "yes" wasn't just a sales skill, it could change everything. For most of my life, I had felt powerless, stripped of control. But here in the showroom, I finally saw an opportunity to grasp power over my own destiny.

I had barely managed to wrap my head around the basics when a small miracle happened. A customer walked into the dealership, interested in Hyundai vehicles. I'd been listening to my colleagues' advice and studying their techniques, so with my heart pounding, I decided to seize the moment. The customer asked to look at some Hyundais, and my mind raced as I tried to recall the names of the models. In a split-second panic, I blurted out, "Would you like to see a Civic?" (The Civic was a Honda, of course; not a Hyundai.)

It was a big blunder and a stark demonstration of my glaring lack of knowledge. And somehow, despite the blunder, I was able to make the sale.

The exhilaration of that day didn't just fill my pockets with a commission; it ignited a fire inside me. I began to see that every "no" I encountered was just a steppingstone to a "yes," and every rejection was a challenge waiting to be met with an even stronger effort. I immersed myself in the world of sales with a passion and a hunger I'd never known before. I would stay late after my shifts, poring over brochures and manuals, trying to memorize all the essential details. I'd sit in on meetings with senior salespeople, scribbling notes and asking questions that sometimes made me feel foolish. But every mistake was a lesson, and a building block for the future I desperately wanted to construct.

Mornings at the dealership were anything but ordinary. The sun was rising outside, and inside the showroom, it was a stage to perform on. The smell hit you first: Cologne that tried to cover up yesterday's liquor, burnt coffee, and the sharp, synthetic tang of prescription stimulants. Guys stumbled in with wrinkled dress shirts and bloodshot eyes, their ties knotted hastily, sunglasses still on, some still buzzing from the night before. It wasn't uncommon to see a line of white powder vanish from a phone screen right there on the bathroom counter, or a bottle of Adderall being passed around like breath mints. There was no judgment, just a quest for success. Everyone was chasing the same high: closing the next deal, beating the board, being seen, making money. Money.

Then came the meetings. They were loud, volatile, and intense. It didn't matter if you were hungover or half-dead, you were expected to sit up straight and nod like your life depended on it, because in a way, it did. Managers stormed in like drill sergeants on a bender, hurling threats, flipping mini-fridges, slamming phone books on desks. They screamed until their faces turned purple, calling us soft, calling us broke, daring us to prove we belonged. The business model wasn't motivation, it was intimidation. We were being groomed to sell with our backs against the wall, to turn every "no" into a personal insult and every "yes" into an adrenaline shot. They didn't want thinkers, they wanted killers. Closers. Sharks. And we played along, because sharks keep swimming or they die.

During that time, every sale and every customer interaction was charged with the promise of something more: groceries, a roof over my head, a future that didn't involve dumpster diving to survive. It was driving me to succeed, and the more I succeeded, the more the other salespeople hated me. It's lonely at the top, as they say. They often made jokes about me having a "horseshoe up my ass." I wasn't the polished, well-educated salesman, but I was relentless, passionate, and eager to improve.

My life experience of surviving the streets, prison, bars – and always finding a way – had taught me a certain set of skills. Those Grinnell classes probably didn't hurt.

It turned out that, that particular mix, plus my ADHD and personality, could be converted directly into car sales.

I spent all the time that I wasn't selling by obsessing over every interaction, every misstep, and every victory, determined to understand my own shortcomings. I had something to prove.

I had moments when the weight of my past seemed unbearable, when the ghosts of my mistakes whispered that I didn't belong here. But each time, I just made another sale. Each set of keys handed to a new owner was a step away from the dumpster and toward a future I had yet to fully comprehend.

Within two months, I was the top salesperson in the dealership, and within six months, I ranked in the top one percent of BMW salespeople in the nation.

The day they handed me the keys to my first brand new BMW demo car was surreal. I was still living in the homeless shelter. So every evening after work, I was driving a brand new luxury car back to a homeless shelter to sleep.

30

WELCOME TO THE JUNGLE

We were a tribe of misfits dressed in shiny shoes and skinny ties, bonded not by blood but by the grind of the asphalt jungle. I had new people.

For many of us, myself especially, those long days of bright lights, metal desks, and ringing phones formed a family. It was a dysfunctional family, to be sure, a warped brotherhood shaped by competition and surviving by selling. Sharks keep swimming. We didn't clock out and go back to our wives or bowling leagues. We stayed in the mess together, grabbed late-night steaks, chased highs, shared bar tabs, swapped war stories, and looked out for one another. None of us really had friends outside the dealership. We were one another's world, for better or worse.

Our friendship was forged on the sales floor and it was sponsored by Adderall. We were too sleep-deprived, too jacked-up, too prideful to say we loved each other, but our twisted traditions said it for us. On birthdays, it was open season: You'd get tackled, hogtied with duct tape, and, if you put up a fight – God help you – you'd get zapped with a taser and thrown into the back of a dealer pickup. The drive-through car wash was the grand finale, hot wax searing your skin while your so-called "brothers" howled with laughter from the cab. Once when a new car manager joined the crew, we broke into his house at night – five of us, drunk and determined – and disassembled every stick of furniture he owned. Every nut, every bolt. It took us hours. His wife was livid. He was flattered. That was our way of welcoming someone to the family.

Behind all the pranks and profanity, there was another rule: Sell or be eaten alive. You could snort a line of cocaine off the conference table, sleep with a stripper, or punch a teammate in the face, but if your numbers slipped, so did your status. Respect was earned not by character, but by closing ratios. If you were killing it, you were king, even if everyone hated you for beating them. I knew that hate well. I felt it burn in their sideways glances and passive jabs. But we all hated one another a little, because we were mirrors reflecting the truth of what we really were.

I was out of the shelter, living with another guy on the sales team. We had a house together and once again, I had the party spot.

My success came with its own set of challenges. The pressure to stay on top was immense, and I began to look for ways to keep up my energy and focus. At first, I turned to the Adderall that was so easily at hand. It gave me the edge I needed to outwork everyone else, but it wasn't long before I needed more to achieve the same effect. Cocaine followed, and for the first time in my life, I had money to burn. It disappeared as quickly as I earned it, spent on more drugs, expensive dinners, and chasing women.

31

THE WATER COOLER

I remember one night clearly. After a long day at the dealership, a few of us salespeople climbed into a BMW 7 Series along with my sales manager, Rick, and our finance manager, Lynn. We ended up a few miles away outside The Water Cooler, the bar where I'd found another form of family after another stint between prisons.

The Water Cooler isn't the kind of place you go to see and be seen for a martini. It's not some classy pub where nice people meet old friends over craft beers. It is the kind of place you gravitate toward when you don't care who sees you spiraling.

It is a living, breathing paradox. It is a low-ceilinged shack, a bunker for the broken, the wild, and the worn-out. It has an energy you could feel before you ever opened the door, but not a positive one. A heavy, deep, dark, sucking energy. The air always smells of cigarettes, spilled beer, and the body odor rolling off people teetering on the edge. Inside, there were no rules, only clinking bottles, jukebox anthems, sad confessions, and sudden shouts. It was a hut for the wrecked and the reckless. That's why I liked it. Nobody cared who you were, what you'd done, or how badly you were unraveling. You could drink yourself into oblivion, start a fight, get dragged out back, and then stumble right back in the next night like nothing had happened. It was loud, always loud. Music pounded from a half-broken jukebox playing everything from outlaw country to gangster rap, often overlapping with a drunken rendition of someone screaming their heartbreak into the karaoke mic.

There was no bouncer, no cameras, no rules. If a fight broke out, which it did often, people just shuffled their drinks out of the way and let the chaos unfold. Sometimes blood hit the floor before the whiskey glass did. But call the cops? That was laughable. If the cops ever came, it wouldn't be to save anyone, it would be to drag half the place to jail. Everyone knew that, so they handled their business in-house. The Water Cooler wasn't safe. It wasn't warm. But it was loyal in its own twisted way. A confessional booth for the damned. A sanctuary for people who had long stopped asking for salvation.

And in the middle of all this beautiful madness was Joab. Joab wasn't just the manager of the place, he was the glue of it. He had eyes that never missed anything. He didn't just tolerate the chaos, he orchestrated it. Joab had this uncanny way of seeing people. He saw their essence and somehow made them feel seen without feeling judged. He could throw out a heckler, break up a brawl, and have a vulnerable heart-to-heart all in the same hour.

I met him one night and from that moment on, something clicked. He had a magnetic personality: witty, disarming, and very intelligent. In a place where most of us were barely holding ourselves together, Joab made us feel like we belonged. Like maybe the broken could be beautiful if they broke together.

As we drove through the dark streets, Rick pulled out a small bag of white powder. With a steady hand, he laid a neat line on the center console. I hesitated for just a moment then leaned in and snorted the line. Almost immediately, a rush of energy coursed through me, a sudden feeling of power and control that made me forget everything else for a brief moment.

As the cocaine hit my bloodstream, it felt like someone had flipped a switch and I was now seeing the world in high definition. My chest tightened, not in a painful way, but like it had just been supercharged. Every sound became sharper, every light more intense. My confidence surged like a tidal wave crashing through my insecurities, and for a moment, I wasn't broken; I was invincible. I was the smartest, funniest guy in the room, even if I wasn't saying anything at all. The shame, the wreckage, the inner noise got drowned out by a symphony of euphoria. The rush was fast and loud, like lighting a fuse that explodes instantly and leaves you standing in the smoke, laughing without knowing why.

But thirty minutes later, what that fuse had lit fizzled into an empty ache. It didn't crash like heroin or lull like booze; it itched. A restless hunger curled into my brain, whispering *more.* Not because I needed to get high again, but because I couldn't stand going back to normal. Normal was too quiet. Too slow. Too real. So I chased that feeling, line after line, always trying to catch up to the magic of the first one. And each time, the return was a little shorter, a little dimmer, until all that was left was the ritual. The mirror, the blade, the line. I wasn't high anymore. I was just trying not to feel low.

But in the first moment that I did my first line, I felt like I was part of an inner circle, a secret world where the rules were different. The shared act bonded us together; it was as if Rick,

Lynn, and I were in on something that most people would never experience. The feeling wasn't just about the high, it was about belonging, and the little orphan inside of me was always looking for that.

The car sales and cocaine phase was a loop that was fast, reckless, and barely tethered. More nights than I care to count ended with me passed out in the front seat of my demo car, slouched like a discarded jacket, the smell of stale cologne, sweat, and liquor soaking into the fabric. These weren't luxurious moments in a borrowed car; they were pit stops on the edge of another inevitable crash. I'd park somewhere out of sight behind the dealership, windows fogged from my breath, a crumpled hoodie balled up as a pillow, and hope that the sunrise would wake me before my managers did.

The mornings came with no mercy. One of the other sales guys, usually half amused, half annoyed, would tap on the glass, smirking as I startled awake, eyes bloodshot, tongue dry, heart already racing from the leftover chemicals in my system. I'd stumble into the building through the service entrance, dodging side eyes, and head straight for the bathroom. I'd scrub my face, run a wet paper towel through my hair, and switch into "professional" mode. Or at least something I thought was close enough. A quick bump of coke off a key, a few deep breaths, and I was back out on the floor selling dreams with four wheels. It became a miserable routine that I knew might kill me, but I didn't care.

I was dealer of the month, had money in my pocket and women on my arm, and I felt invincible. I was the guy everyone either wanted to be or couldn't stand. My name carried weight in every meeting. I swaggered through the showroom, and I moved through life like it owed me something.

I'd managed to stay out of jail for nearly two years … which is not to say I hadn't done anything that could land me there. And underneath that loud, fast, money-drenched climb, the foundation was still cracked and broken and my basement was flooding again. And when it gave way, it didn't warn me. It swallowed me whole.

Perhaps it would have happened faster if it hadn't been for Bart Woods. Steady, stable, wise Bart who was offering me something better.

We used to meet for lunch, Bart and I.

I had asked him to be my mentor maybe a year before those lunches became routine. Bart was a prominent business owner, a respected community leader, a father and husband, but more than anything else, he was a man of God. That order of importance mattered to him: God, husband, father, community, business.

I came to him because I wanted help becoming successful. I wanted strategies, systems, wisdom that would move the needle. He came to me because he cared about my hurt and about my relationship with Christ.

That mismatch used to frustrate me.

I would ask him specific questions about business, about growth, about decisions I thought were urgent, and he would gently slide past them and circle right back to my heart. Back to my faith. Back to who I was becoming. At the time, I remember thinking he was avoiding the practical stuff, the things I thought really mattered. Looking back, my sense is that his motive was twofold. First, he genuinely cared about where I would spend eternity. Second, he had no interest in helping someone build success without character, because success like that is not sustainable, and maybe not even worth having. I never asked him outright, and I do not want to put words in his mouth, but that was the sense I carried away from those lunches.

One day, while I was on break, we met at a local neighborhood restaurant, a little cafe known for the best burger in town. I sat across from Bart, probably whining about some situation I had created myself. At the time, I'm sure that whatever it was felt very real to me, very big, and very unfair. I always wore my frustration like a badge of victimhood. Bart sat there patiently, looking at me like I was the most important person in the world. Not glancing at his phone. Not rushing the moment. Fully present.

What Bart did not know was that I knew something about him.

Even though I was still a mess in many ways, I had become fairly connected in the community by then. I knew that he was dealing with something big, something that would have completely rocked most men. A deal he was involved in had gone sideways in a major way. Even though it was not his fault, it was going to affect him financially in a significant way. It was the kind of situation that keeps people up at night, the kind that tightens your chest and steals your peace every waking moment AND while you sleep.

I never mentioned it. I never let on that I knew.

Neither did he.

While I complained about my petty problem, he was dealing with the weight of the world, and he never let on.

What stayed with me was not the advice he gave that day, or the questions he asked, but the way he carried himself. The way he listened. The way he made space for my small, self-created problems while he was quietly carrying something of his own that was devastating.

Bart is steady. Bart is calm. It's a calm that did not make sense to me at the time. I remember thinking, how can someone have this much peace in the middle of a storm like that?

What does he know that I do not know? Or better yet, *who does he know*?

Is this because of this Jesus he keeps trying to tell me about?

Watching him walk through that season planted a seed in me that did not result in immediate change. No instant turn-around from that lunch. But the seed lodged itself deep inside. It made me ask deeper questions, not just about success, but about peace, character, and the kind of life that can stand firm when the ground underneath it starts to shift.

I wish the shift had come sooner, but it didn't.

My collapse didn't look like a crash at first, it looked like success turning sour in slow motion. I started losing the edge. Deals got sloppy. People I thought were friends started backing off, watching like spectators at a train wreck they didn't want to admit they saw coming. Cocaine stopped being a party favor and started being a requirement. Sleep became optional. The lies I told others started bleeding into the ones I told myself. Then came the breakdowns.

The tiny empire I built in my mind wasn't made of stone, it was made of expensive white dust. And that dust finally settled.

32

TWENTY-SIX SHOTS

The night I got shot by the police should have been the moment everything changed. For most people, a near-death experience sparks some kind of epiphany, doesn't it?

Aren't you supposed to get a realization that life is fleeting, that things have to change?

For me, it only confirmed what I already believed: Life was cruel, chaotic, empty and out to get me. I had built an entire narrative around my own pain, a masterclass in self-deception so convincing that I believed it completely. Every betrayal I committed, every bridge I torched, I boarded over as someone else's injustice against me.

I wasn't the liar; I was misunderstood.

I wasn't the manipulator; I was just reacting to a world that had broken me.

But beneath the surface of that story – with my trembling lips, wounded gaze, and long list of excuses – was a more troubling truth: I wasn't the victim. I was the abuser.

Looking back now, it's almost chilling to see how well I played the part. I knew how to cry at the right moment, how to turn a confrontation into a pity party. I'd talk about my trauma as if it gave me a free pass to cause trauma. I weaponized my wounds. I could charm a room, beg forgiveness, and cast myself as the one always getting hurt while simultaneously tearing people apart emotionally, financially, and spiritually. That's the twisted part: I thought I was the hero in a survival story, but I was really a devouring plague.

And no one could hold me accountable.

Instead of a wake-up call, those twenty-six shots fired were a free fall into a darker abyss.

Here's how I got there.

It was March, somewhere around 2 a.m. and the city is mostly asleep, except for people like me. Streetlights hum. Roads empty. The world is quiet enough that if you're wrestling with demons, they sound loud. There's nothing to drown them out.

I was driving my store demo, a brand-new BMW M4, orange on orange, a car the dealership had handed me for being top salesman. I had just picked up Ellie. Up until then, she had been a fling, nothing rooted, nothing safe. I had dated her cousin once. Life was messy like that. I had been drinking throughout the night. I was angry, not in a way that made sense, not at one thing or one person. It was heavier and uglier.

I had once been homeless. Now I had a chance, a real one, and I was killing it on paper. I was making good money. I was driving a car most guys my age only saw on posters. And yet I never felt like I was getting ahead. I wanted to be a winner and I wanted to be a partier. I wanted to settle down and I wanted to stay unfaithful. I wanted connection but could not be trusted. I wanted to slow down and go faster at the same time.

I had believed money would fix everything. Instead, it amplified everything. My arrogance grew alongside my insecurity.

Somewhere after picking Ellie up, the tunnel vision set in. That familiar narrowing of the world. I wanted control. I needed to feel it. And I was sitting in a machine designed to reward recklessness. The engine roared. The car begged to be pushed. And I gave myself over to its request.

I peeled around corners, tires screaming, the motor revving like it shared my instability. Cedar Rapids was mostly empty, wide open, and I treated it like a private track. In the back of my mind, a quieter voice kept whispering that I should slow down. That I should just go home. That this never ends well.

But I could not stop.

Then the lights appeared behind me. Red and blue, flashing in the rearview mirror. I flipped on my turn signal, pretending, maybe even convincing myself, that I was about to pull over. For a brief moment, I thought I would.

Until the last second.

Instead I mashed the gas.

I took a right. Then another right. I punched the gas hard and felt the distance open between me and the squad car. I turned left down a one-way street, the wrong way, the kind of decision that feels inevitable once you have already crossed a certain line. Over the radio, they called a do-not-pursue. I did not know that then. I just kept going.

I turned up a steep incline into an alley, just three blocks from my house. Three blocks from safety, or so I thought. I eased forward, creeping toward the end of the alley, my heart pounding, my hands tight on the wheel. I thought I'd lost them.

Then another squad car emerged.

They backed up and came straight at me, filling the alley, blocking my exit. Instinct took over. Panic. Survival. I threw the car into reverse and floored it. Forty-five miles per hour in an alley. Sirens. Lights bouncing off brick walls. The world collapsed into sound and color.

The crash came hard. I backed straight into a telephone pole at forty-five miles an hour. Metal folded. Airbags exploded. For a split second, everything stopped.

I opened my eyes, trapped by police on both sides.

I saw a way out.

Could I squeeze around the cop car in front of me, between it and the fence?

Maybe.

We'd see.

I hit the gas and spun the wheel around the police car in front of me, trying to squeeze past, to escape the consequences I had been outrunning my entire life.

That's when they opened fire.

Twenty-six rounds.

Glass exploded inward, raining down like violent confetti. Ellie screamed. Voices shouted commands. "Get out of the car! Get out of the car!"

Time fractured. My body locked. I could not move.

Hands ripped me from the wreckage. I hit the ground. Pain registered dull and distant.

As the cold pavement pressed into my cheek and the world began to fade, one final thought cut through the chaos, quiet and terrifying in its clarity.

"Is this it?"

And then everything went black.

The physical pain was nothing compared to what came after. From the hospital to the police station, everything blurred together into a haze of agony and fear.

To make the shooting sting even worse, it happened in my demo. Not just any demo, but a brand new, fire-breathing BMW M4 in a head-turning orange-on-orange spec. It was the kind of car that made jaws drop at gas stations and had strangers pulling out their phones to take photos. Its burnt orange paint glistened like molten lava under the sun, while the interior was wrapped in a matching blaze of stitched leather: loud, proud, and unapologetically flashy … just like me. It was a rolling billboard that screamed to everyone that I had arrived, even if the truth was that I was barely holding it all together.

That illusion was shredded in seconds. Twenty-six bullet holes tore through that car like it was paper. The windshield splintered, the doors looked like swiss cheese, and blood pooled against the glowing interior like a gruesome piece of modern art. The bright leather soaked it in. I still remember the ear-splitting ring of each shot as it pierced the metal, and the way the engine ticked as it cooled. It wasn't just the destruction of a demo car. It signaled the end of my whole destructive, chaotic performance.

The next thing I remember came in fragments, a blurry haze from shock and drugs and trauma.

Light.

Voices.

Motion.

I came to for a moment while being rushed toward the emergency room, then I slipped back out of consciousness. The ceiling above me moved fast, panels and fluorescent lights blurring together. Someone was shouting numbers. Someone else was shouting my name. I could feel hands on my body, firm and urgent, pressing, holding, cutting away fabric. Then the darkness pulled me back down again.

I surfaced once more as the doors burst open.

The operating room hit me all at once. The smell first. That unmistakable OR smell, antiseptic and metal and something human. The air felt cold.

Brighter.

Louder. We busted through those doors like the horrors of the alleyway had followed us inside.

People were already waiting. Doctors. Nurses. Scrubs. Moving fast, practiced, calm. Practiced. I was still on the gurney, still bleeding, still drifting in and out, but I could feel the shift. From street chaos to clinical urgency.

From blaring sirens to the surgeon's commands.

"Gunshot wounds."

"Three."

"BP dropping."

I remember faces leaning over me, then sliding out of view. I remember someone squeezing my shoulder, grounding me just enough to keep me here. I remember the sting of something sharp, then nothing again.

Police were there. Dark blue uniforms in the corners of my vision. Standing against the wall. Watching. Waiting. Even then, even half conscious, I knew I was not just a patient. I was evidence. I was a liability.

They cut my clothes off. The same clothes I had been wearing just hours earlier, when I was invincible. Fabric fell to the floor somewhere near my feet. I felt exposed in every possible way. My body was broken open. My life split wide.

I drifted again.

When I came back, they were still working on me. Monitors beeping in steady rhythms. The ceiling lights burned my eyes. My mouth felt dry, like I had been screaming for days even though I could not remember making a sound.

Pain tried to rise, but it was muted, held at bay by chemicals and shock. What remained was confusion. Disorientation. The strange awareness that I was alive when I probably should not have been.

I remember thinking, not clearly, "This is what it looks like when everything finally catches up, Kyle."

When all the bad decisions, all the arrogance, all the running pile into one room.

I faded in and out as they stabilized me, stitched me, plugged holes I should not survive. Each time I slipped away, I wondered if I would come back again. Each time I did, the same thought hovered just out of reach.

How did I get here?

The answer was everywhere around me.

Another truth was forming.

I was still alive.

At the police station, I was confined to a wheelchair and handcuffed. Every movement I attempted was an agonizing reminder of the pain I was in. I was exhausted from surgery and my body was begging for sleep, yet I was too scared to let my guard down.

I couldn't believe what had happened; the disbelief was overwhelming. I had messed up so badly, and every thought churned through me like another dark, relentless, emotional storm. The minutes stretched into hours as I sat in a boiling mixture of shock, regret, and raw anger swirling through my mind. It was as if I were trapped in a bad dream, unable to wake up or escape the memories that played out over and over.

Despite the pain and fatigue, I lashed out at anyone who crossed me. I was belligerent and combative, like a dog backed into a corner. My years of pent-up hatred toward the police, which had simmered quietly for so long, suddenly erupted into an all-consuming fury. I demanded to know what charges I was facing, my voice echoing off the walls of the station as I screamed.

Instead of getting the answers I so desperately wanted, I was met with silence and indifference. No one would tell me what I was being charged with. My anger began to give way to bitter resignation. Then, without the confrontation I expected, I was simply released from police custody. Released.

I was more confused than ever.

33

LET'S GET YOU HOME

A cop gave me a ride home. My car was impounded as evidence and obviously not drivable. My phone was confiscated too, leaving me completely cut off. Isolated.

But they had let me go.

It sounds insane, I know, it might even seem untrue, but it's not.

One minute I'm handcuffed on the asphalt, bleeding from bullet wounds, adrenaline surging through my body ... and the next, I'm sitting in the back of a cop car with no cuffs, no guard, no charges. Just a vague statement that the Department of Criminal Investigation (DCI) would be handling things from here. In the aftermath of a police-involved shooting, that kind of limbo isn't as rare as it sounds. The local cops are told to stand down while the DCI steps in to sort out what happened ... what *really* happened. So there I was: rattled, sore, stitched up, and technically free.

The other unbelievable truth is that it feels like something like this would take days. It all unfolded over hours. I'd been slumped in blood in an alley at 2 a.m., and by 10 a.m. I was being driven to my doorstep.

205

John was the DCI agent assigned to my case. I expected a guy with that job to be cold, maybe even hostile; some steely-eyed badge looking to bury you. But John wasn't that. He was calm. Gentle eyes, a sort of weary compassion I didn't expect. I'm sure he had seen a lot over the years. He didn't treat me like a monster. He treated me like a man who'd been through hell and might still be trying to crawl out. That threw me off.

The ride in his cruiser was quiet except for the hum of the heater trying to keep the winter chill at bay. My mind raced from the pain I was feeling and the growing realization of what awaited me at home. My house wasn't just a place to sleep; it was a trap house. I hadn't even remembered the mountain of cocaine covering the kitchen table until we reached the steps to my front door. That's when panic set in.

John glanced at me as he turned off the engine. "You good?" he asked, his tone mostly neutral but tinged with some suspicion.

"Yeah, I just need help getting up the steps," I muttered, avoiding his eyes. He got out and walked around the car to help.

He didn't say much as he helped me out of the unmarked cruiser. The frigid winter air blew right through the hospital scrubs I still wore. My body was wrecked – torn open, stitched together, and barely functional – but I was home. Free, for now. But I couldn't make it inside the house on my own.

John looped one of my arms over his shoulder and all but carried me, one agonizing step at a time, up the concrete stairs. I tried to help by pushing with what little strength I had in my legs, but it felt like someone was grinding glass under my skin with every movement. My breath caught with each jolt.

At the top, he eased me onto the porch and told me to stay put. My wheelchair had slid backward in the trunk of the cruiser, and he had to wrestle it free. When he returned with the chair, he helped me into it and we paused again, both breathing heavily but for different reasons. The front door was just inches away; I reached for it but then hesitated. My heart pounded because of the pile of white truth that I knew waited inside. That table with the mountain of cocaine spread across it was a careless display of my collapse and my guilt.

Before he reached for the door, John looked at me sharply. He had seen my sudden stop and the split-second look of panic on my face. His instincts were on high alert, and he asked me in a low voice, "Is there any bomb-making material on the other side of this door?" I shook my head. "No," I croaked, barely above a whisper. He nodded, then continued without emotion. "All right. I'll give you a pass." And just like that, mercy prevailed over police protocol. He pushed the door open and moved the table aside, sending lines of cocaine scattering. Without a word, he cleared a path for my wheelchair as I watched him, stunned by his humanity shown in that one strange, unforgettable moment.

True to his word, nothing ever came of it. Maybe he pitied me, or maybe he thought I'd already been through enough that night. Whatever the reason, I didn't argue.

34

TORMENT

The days that followed were a waking nightmare. The physical pain from my injuries was intense and relentless, as well as a constant reminder of how close I'd come to dying. I never sought follow-up care after the surgery. It's not really because I was trying to be tough, but because I was drowning in chaos. My life back then wasn't built for responsibility or recovery. I didn't have the bandwidth to think ahead, let alone find a doctor, navigate insurance, or schedule appointments. I was more focused on numbing the pain than treating it. My priorities were survival and sedation, anything to keep the noise quiet, even if just for an hour or two.

Oddly enough, the one who ended up tending to my wounds was an ex-girlfriend, Nancy, who was a nurse, and who also had every reason to never speak to me again. Our relationship and inevitable breakup had been as messy as my life in cocaine and cars, but despite the bitterness she felt toward me, she was a nurse and she showed up. She didn't sugarcoat how stupid she thought I was, and she was clinical, even cold toward me. But she was also careful, and she sat me down and pulled the stitches out with a precision that came from her years of experience. Although her touch was detached, I felt the grace that surprises you when you know you're too wrecked to deserve it.

The emotional and mental toll of the shooting was worse than the physical pain. My job was gone, of course. The dealership wasted no time cutting ties with me. The sharks kept swimming without me, and once again, the people who I thought were my friends vanished, leaving me feeling isolated and bitter. I spent most days alone, because the police had taken my phone as evidence and I didn't have any way to reach anyone, including Ellie, who had been in the car. I couldn't walk, so I just hung out steeped in self-pity.

In the midst of the chaos following the shooting and all the subsequent fallout, the media barrage, the haunting silence from the police station, and the searing regret of my actions, one person unexpectedly became a pillar of support: my friend Sam. Although we hadn't been particularly close while we were selling cars together, something changed after the incident. Sam began checking on me regularly, reaching out at a time when I was drowning in a sea of pain and self-loathing. His presence was a small but powerful reminder that I wasn't entirely alone in my struggle.

Sam's support extended far beyond mere check-ins. He took me fishing on quiet mornings when the world seemed to be closing in on me, offering a gentle respite from the storm of my thoughts. He even took me to a comedy night, where laughter, which I hadn't expressed in a long time, started to crack through the darkness. It wasn't just the outings themselves, but the genuine care behind them that made all the difference. In those moments, as I sat by the water or laughed at a punchline, his friendship offered some hope amid the pain.

Perhaps one of the most significant gestures of Sam's friendship was when he gave me a dog named Nala. An American Bully with the stature of a show champion and the eyes of an old soul, Nala carried herself like royalty but loved in a way I hadn't known before. Dog owners will get this. I didn't know I needed her until the moment she pressed her head into my chest like she already knew where I was hurting. She laid at the foot of my bed, alert to every wince and groan that came with the slow process of healing.

Nala had once competed in arenas under spotlights, all eyes on her as she strutted with practiced perfection. She was with me when I took my first steps again. She was fiercely loyal. In a world where everyone had written me off, Nala wanted to be near.

Today, Sam and I remain great friends, united by our shared journey of healing and redemption. Though he, too, had his share of struggles and was still finding his way when we first reconnected, his genuine nature shone through, and I could tell he was maturing. Now, following the Lord together, I watch in awe as God has radically transformed his life. Sam is now the proud father of three beautiful daughters and the owner of a successful construction company, a testament to his character and the power of Jesus to restore those who come to Him.

But I get ahead of myself again.

35

GIRLS, GIRLS, GIRLS

Before the gunshots shattered the night and turned everything upside down, my life at the car dealership was already a slow-motion wreck. You wouldn't have known it from the outside. On paper, I was winning. Selling cars, stacking money, always flashing a new watch or pulling up in a fresh demo. I had a devil-may-care grin and I projected the confidence of a man who thought he had it all figured out. But underneath the hustle and charm was something ugly, a rot that spread through every relationship I touched.

I wasn't looking for commitment. I was looking for someone to soothe the constant ache in my chest that came from growing up without a real family. I had a hollow space where stability and unconditional love should've been.

I thought if I could just find the right girl, the perfect one, she'd make me feel whole. But that's the thing: Broken people don't heal by leaning on other broken people, and I didn't want healing anyway. I wanted anesthesia. So I lied. I manipulated. I cheated. I left when I got bored. When one woman couldn't carry the weight of my chaos, I'd move on to the next, always convincing myself that *this one* might finally fix me.

That was the headspace I was in when Ellie came into the picture.

At first, Ellie was just easy. She was down for "whatever," and she didn't ask questions I didn't want to answer. She was soft-spoken, and she had kind eyes and a sadness behind her smile that felt familiar. We didn't have deep talks or plans for the future, we just did whatever felt good in the moment, numbing each other with whatever vice was available. I never expected her to stick around. She was a background character in my chaotic life, someone to text when the night felt too quiet.

Around that time, there was another girl too, Jody.

Now Jody was different.

She was extra sharp, ambitious, and, if I'm being honest, way out of my league. She saw through the act. Maybe that's why I wanted her so badly. She played a game I couldn't master. Some nights, I was the star in her sky. Other nights, she didn't even acknowledge I existed. And even though it drove me insane, deep down I knew I was just getting a taste of my own poison. She was doing to me what I had done to so many others.

The night I got shot, I was chasing that hollow ache again. I swung by the bar where Jody worked, hoping she would throw me a bone, something to keep my pride intact. But she shut me down, cold and decisive. So I did what I always did: I fell back into what was comfortable and familiar. I called Ellie.

We got wasted. Reckless. I don't even remember what I was running from that night, but I remember the way I drove. I drove like nothing mattered. Like I was daring the world to hit back. And eventually, it did.

Sirens. Lights. Gunfire. Glass shattering and metal twisting. Ellie screaming beside me. My blood painting the inside of the car.

It's strange, but that night bound us together in a way that nothing else could have. When everyone else ghosted me: coworkers, friends, people I partied with, Ellie didn't. As my loneliness during recovery stretched on, with Sam and Nala as my only companions, Ellie showed up. And she stayed. She didn't leave. Not for a long time. Maybe it was loyalty. Maybe trauma. Maybe codependency dressed up as love. But she stayed.

She was only nineteen. I was twenty-five. She was beautiful in that fragile, delicate way that made you want to protect her until you realized she didn't think she deserved to be protected. Just like me, she came from a mess of a home, and in some weird way, we mirrored each other's brokenness. I pushed boundaries, and she never pushed back. I spiraled, and she held the camera. It was never healthy.

Neither of us knew what love was. We just knew we didn't want to be alone. That's all it takes to keep two people tangled together and spiraling. And no amount of attention, affection, or loyalty could fix that. Not from Ellie. Not from Jodie. Not from anyone. Because healing doesn't come from using people to fill the void. It comes from facing the void and dealing with it. But I was still sprinting at full speed into the darkness.

Figuratively.

Literally, learning to walk again was my latest daunting challenge. My legs, always reliable, now trembled with the very thought of supporting me. I was so full of dread and confusion: hope for the possibility of recovery, and dread of the sharp, stabbing pain of standing on my legs. The process was painstakingly slow. I really couldn't go to physical therapy. I didn't have the money, or the car, or the mental capacity. The act of walking that once came as naturally as breathing, now required a deliberate, almost ritualistic effort. Every small, shuffling step came in an overwhelming sea of pain and doubt.

It's strange, really, how something so violent, with the potential to be so final, could end up with me walking today with full mobility. I have no lingering limp. No frozen joints. No visible reason for people to have any idea what I've been through. If you didn't know the story, you might never guess I'd been shot at all. And yet, beneath the skin, the story is still there in the form of scar tissue and embedded metal.

The doctors couldn't remove all the fragments from my leg. One bullet shattered into a constellation of pieces. Somehow, by some miracle, none of the pieces hit an artery or severed a nerve. I should've been crippled; I should've lost a limb, if not my life. But I didn't. It's like God Himself reached down and guided those bullets just enough to spare me.

I don't say that lightly. There's no medical reason I should've come out the other side the way I did. I'm not just lucky. I was protected for a purpose.

The bullet that is still in my upper leg doesn't hurt. I barely notice it anymore. But sometimes I remember it's there. And I think about how close I came to never walking again. Never holding my daughter. Never finding redemption. That bullet inside me? It's a silent witness to a dead man named Kyle Orth.

In addition to my body healing, my mind and emotions were trying to heal also. I must have had PTSD. I was so badly paranoid. Every creak or rustle in the dark was magnified into an ominous threat. Any noise made my heart race, and I found myself trapped in a state of hyper-vigilance. Even the sight of a police car would send shivers down my spine.

The day after I was shot, the media descended on my front lawn like a swarm. Reporters crowded, their cameras ready and their microphones thrust forward, demanding an explanation. Their voices overlapped with urgent questions and speculative headlines. I remember feeling trapped in a surreal moment, torn between the instinct to defend myself and the overwhelming urge to disappear from the spotlight.

Inside, I was in a state of deep conflict. On one hand, I wanted to explain what had happened to give my side of the story and justify my actions. On the other, a paralyzing sense of shame and fear made every public appearance feel like a betrayal of my own privacy. I was suffocating in the realization that, in that moment just before I was shot, my selfishness had blinded me to the danger I posed not only to myself but also to Ellie and to the officers involved.

With time, the truth became clear: My actions were indefensible. I had endangered lives, compromised the safety of those around me, and, in a moment of reckless abandon, betrayed the trust of an employer who had given me a second chance I didn't deserve. The stark reality of that day was hard to face, as I recognized the full measure of my irresponsibility and the lasting impact it had on everyone connected to that incident.

Social media only amplified the turmoil. Facebook became a forum where every past slight was discussed and debated.

Every woman I had treated poorly over the previous years used the incident to air out her grievances publicly. Their posts, passionate and unfiltered, painted a picture of a man whose past actions had come back to haunt him. I didn't blame them. If anything, I knew deep down that I had been a jerk and that I deserved every bit of their anger.

Then there were the voices of strangers and people who barely knew me but felt compelled to demand justice and offer their own theories on why I ran from the police. Their words cut deep and were a reminder that public opinion can be as unforgiving as it is swift. In the midst of the clamor, I was forced to confront the reality that my life had spiraled into a spectacle; a cautionary tale of self-destruction, where every misstep was magnified under the unforgiving glare of the media and the court of public opinion.

I was struggling to recover physically and emotionally, and I was also thrust into a legal nightmare that exposed the realities of our judicial system. Throughout my life, I had been represented by public defenders, perhaps bright but tragically overworked and underfunded. They did the best they could with limited resources, often forced into accepting quick settlements or plea bargains that were something kind of like what passes for justice. I had a sense of bitter injustice and thought that the system was rigged against people like me.

But, in a twist of fate, I connected with a defense lawyer in Cedar Rapids who was arguably the best defense attorney in the area. Recognizing the potential to build a landmark case by suing the police for the shooting, and garnering the publicity that would come with it, he offered to represent me pro bono. Unlike the public defenders who had been my only recourse in the past, he came equipped with a full arsenal of resources and expertise, and a strong desire to challenge the status quo (and make a name for himself). His approach was bold and unrelenting, a stark contrast to the constrained, survival-focused tactics of my previous legal representatives.

My legal journey illuminated a painful truth: There are two very different judicial systems at play. On one hand, you have the public defender system, designed for those who simply cannot afford a private attorney. Despite their dedication, public defenders are stretched thin, often dealing with overwhelming caseloads that leave little room for the in-depth investigation and personalized strategy that a case like mine demanded. On the other hand, the private legal sphere offers a level of advocacy that is unattainable without financial means, where a top-tier lawyer can craft strategies, work with a team, and pursue justice at a level that the under-resourced system simply cannot.

Let me say it again plainly: The legal system we experience depends on whether we have money or not. It is not the same for everyone.

Having this exceptional lawyer by my side was like being thrown another life preserver in a storm at sea.

As I started to regain mobility, the crushing reality of my financial situation set in. My money was gone, and the bills were piling up. Back when I was selling cars, I rode high on the thrill of easy money. There were months when I'd rake in as much as $30,000 – a windfall that made me feel invincible. But that surge of cash was long gone, blown on wild nights and endless indulgence.

As I had risen out of homelessness, I hadn't learned any kind of practical financial management skills. A vicious cycle of earning and spending left me perpetually broke. No sooner had I earned a big sum than it vanished into the night, blown on expensive bar tabs, numbing drugs, and fleeting moments with women.

After the shooting, after the job was gone and the phone stopped ringing, there was a gnawing urgency in my gut. Survival mode kicked in. Not the kind of survival where you hunt and gather, but the kind where your pride is already on life support and you start weighing morality against desperation. Rent didn't care that I was limping around on a bullet-shattered leg; it demanded to be paid. So Ellie and I, two bruised spirits orbiting one another, slipped into a rhythm we both knew wasn't sustainable, but at least it kept the lights on.

36

ON THE ROAD

There are parts of my story that are too dark to revisit.

It's not that I don't take responsibility for them, I do.

It's that nobody wins for telling them.

So let me sum it up like this: As I recovered physically, things grew far worse for me mentally and spiritually. I didn't have a change of heart, my heart grew very hard.

Ellie and I went on the road. What followed was a delirious, paranoid, criminal run of mistrust and money.

It's complicated, because there was legitimate businesses happening, semi-legitimate business happening, and totally illegal business happening. The lawful business made a front that allowed the illegal stuff to hide.

And then came meth. The first time we used it was in a hotel room in South Bend, Indiana. We were with another couple, people we'd met on the road who seemed to know every shortcut to a good time and every path to destruction. They pulled out the little baggie like it was a sacred offering and my curiosity got the better of me.

Ellie was hesitant, but her meek demeanor made her an easy target for a stronger personality trying to persuade her.

I took the first hit, and it was as if fireworks exploded in my brain. The rush was instantaneous, like nothing I'd ever felt before. It wasn't just a high, it was a revelation. For a brief moment, everything made sense. The noise in my head quieted, and a euphoric clarity took over. I felt invincible, unstoppable, like I could conquer the world!

I stepped outside the hotel, the cold air biting at my skin. The parking lot was littered with trash, the grounds were unkempt, and the building wasn't maintained, but I stood there, staring up at the sky, feeling like I'd unlocked some hidden secret of the universe. Inside, the room reeked, but outside, under the stars, I felt alive. For the first time in years, I felt alive.

For months, meth felt incredible. The highs made everything seem brighter, sharper, and more alive.

Ellie and I felt invincible as we coasted through city after city, our makeshift empire of crime was thriving. But as the days without sleep or real food stretched into weeks without sleep or food, the cracks began to appear. The euphoria faded, replaced by exhaustion and fraying nerves. Our bodies were deteriorating, and so were our minds. Meth had been the answer to everything … until it became the problem we couldn't escape.

The paranoia was the worst part. Innocent shadows became terrifying threats, and any noise was a sign that the cops were closing in. I'd spend hours staring out the windows, convinced we were being watched. The mirrors in our motel rooms became my enemy, reflecting a gaunt, hollow-eyed stranger I barely recognized. Ellie and I fought constantly, our arguments escalating into screaming matches that sometimes turned violent.

Eventually the money stopped mattering. Then everything stopped mattering. All I cared about was the next hit. The drugs altered my mind, feeding delusions and suspicions until I didn't trust anyone, not even myself. I was becoming a monster, consumed by greed, addiction, and paranoia.

Ellie and I spiraled deeper into the madness, our once-functional operation collapsing under the weight of our addictions. The paranoia became unbearable. I'd wake up in the middle of the night, drenched in sweat, convinced the room was surrounded. I started keeping a gun under my pillow, though I didn't even know who or what I was protecting myself from.

Every day blurred into the next. We shuffled from one grimy motel to another, but they all smelled and felt the same. We dragged our misery along with us like a suitcase full of bricks.

The "real" world outside the motel walls was like a distant memory; inside, it was our own special hell. We were no longer living like humans; we were prisoners of our own making, barely surviving. The highs now were never high enough, and the lows became unbearable, each one dragging us further into hell.

Then I met Kristy. Kristy worked the front door at one of the clubs I shouldn't have been frequenting. She wasn't just beautiful, she was arresting: Tall, elegant, fierce, and wrapped in mystery. The first time our eyes locked, something in me changed. The moment marked the beginning of my unraveling. Everything I had built, every ounce of hard-earned street sense and structure I'd put in place to keep my circle safe, I risked for a shot at her attention.

When Kristy moved in, our fling ignited fast and burned reckless. Within weeks, I was breaking my own codes, making exceptions, ignoring red flags that would've once had me hitting the brakes. I thought I was in control, but I was already spiraling. Ellie, who lived with us through it all, became a ghost in the hallway until the shouting started. The house became a war zone. Kristy and I played out a modern-day version of Bonnie and Clyde, except there was no vintage charm or dusty getaway car. just bad decisions, bruised egos, and cops circling like vultures. The violence in our fights was rivaled only by the passion that followed. Each blow, whether physical or emotional, chipped away at the fragile empire I'd built. What started as lust turned into a mine shaft and we were falling down it.

There was no dramatic ending, no fiery climax.

The money was gone.

The drugs were gone.

Ellie was gone.

Kristy was gone.

I was alone at the bottom of a deep, dark hole, addicted to methamphetamines.

37

BETRAYED

Being arrested for a small amount of meth and violating my probation was almost laughable considering the chaos I had been living in and the crimes I'd committed.

In a way, it felt anticlimactic.

With all the laws I'd broken and the havoc I'd wreaked, this was what finally landed me back behind bars? I was lucky, though. It could have been so much worse. Yet, as I sat in the back of the patrol car that night, hands cuffed and heart heavy, I didn't feel lucky. I felt soulless.

I ended up in the Polk County Jail in Des Moines. As I came down off meth in my cell, my mind descended into madness. Sleep became my only escape, and even that was just an empty hiding place. I slept for days, maybe weeks, rising only to choke down the tasteless food I was given, or to stare blankly at the peeling paint on the walls of my cell. My body ached with a sickness that seemed to crawl straight out of my bones, and my mind was in a fog so thick I genuinely wondered if I would ever feel normal again.

Every few hours, I'd wake up with a jolt and a feeling of desperation. I'd shuffle to the phones, my heart pounding with both hope and panic. I'd call whoever I thought might answer, and when someone did, I'd plot, scheme, spin wild promises and manipulations, and try to cobble together enough favor to buy my way out. A few times, it almost worked. I could feel the door cracking open only to have it slam shut at the last second. Each refusal sent me into a deeper free fall. It was a roller coaster of emotion with dizzying highs of false hope and then gut-wrenching plummets of defeat. Suicide felt like the only logical way out. But even that required more strength than I had left. All I could do was lay there half-alive, half-dead waiting to see which side would prevail. Every phone call to a lawyer or a friend led to the same conclusion: I wasn't going anywhere.

Kristy walked into my lawyer's office under the pretense of helping me. She was supposed to write a statement on my behalf, something short but meaningful, a way to toss a line to me when the waters were rising over my head. Instead, she became another piece on a chess board in a game that I did not even know I was playing. And I was a pawn. The lawyer, the man who was supposed to defend me, saw his opening. He knew exactly what I was, a hustler running on fumes. He knew what she was, a beautiful woman with some loneliness and a past. I'd learn later that they became romantically involved.

While I sat in a concrete box counting ceiling cracks and trying to convince myself that I might survive this, he was making moves of his own, moves that pulled Kristy toward him in quiet, calculated ways. By the time I realized what had happened, the damage was done.

I had scraped together $10,000 for my legal defense. It represented every last favor, every swallowed bit of pride I had left. He bled my account until there was nothing left. I was handed off to a frazzled public defender and a legal case no one wanted to touch.

I should have been furious, and part of me was. But mostly I just felt tired, worn thin from the lies, the hustles, the endless scramble for survival. It hit me that I had spent years treating my own life like a sinking ship that I could patch with quick fixes. Now the water was at my chin, and all I could feel was the weight of how long I had been trying to outrun the inevitable.

When the case finally moved forward, it was not with a skilled private lawyer, it was with a public defender who looked tired.

But the truth is, I did not have the strength to care. I was too far gone inside myself. Depression wrapped around me like wet cement. The betrayal hurt the way a bruise hurts when you press on it.

I took the news with my head down, my heart numb, knowing I deserved it. I was tired. Too tired to wonder why the people I trusted kept slipping away. Too tired to ask God why the bottom kept dropping lower.

As I sat there, staring out through the tiny slit of glass in the holding cell door, the reality settled in a new way. The chase was over. The exhausting scramble to stay one step ahead, the endless fight to keep the house of cards from collapsing was finished. There was no money left to buy my way out. No schemes to hatch. No one left to charm or manipulate. It was just me, the cold hard truth, and the heavy acknowledgement that everything had fallen apart.

That was a sliver of relief. For the first time in years, I wasn't running. I wasn't pretending to be someone smarter, tougher, or more invincible than I really was. The walls had closed in, the mask had come off, and all that was left was the broken man underneath. It felt strangely freeing.

After several months of court hearings and negotiations, I pled guilty. The sentence wasn't surprising, but it still stung: prison. Again.

38

ASSAULT & BATTERY

At this point, I was no stranger to Iowa's correctional system. It was routine. My first stop, like everyone else's, was the Iowa Medical and Classification Center (IMCC) in Oakdale. Whether your crime was jaywalking or murder, IMCC was the starting point. This was my seventh time to walk through those gates. Familiarity didn't make it any less repugnant.

For most inmates, IMCC isn't that bad. It's a holding facility where you're assessed and then assigned to a permanent prison. But for those with a history of violence, it's a different story. I'd earned myself a spot in Cell Block B, reserved for the most violent offenders. There, you're on twenty three-hour lockdown, isolated with nothing but your thoughts. The slow march to B Block wasn't something you simply signed up for, it was earned. In the warped economy of prison life, violence was currency, and I'd spent plenty. By the time they moved me to IMCC, my name carried a certain weight in the Iowa Department of Corrections; not respect exactly, but a wary acknowledgment.

B Block wasn't for loudmouths or pretenders; it was reserved for the ones who had proven, time and time again, that they could and would be violent. During my earlier bids, the fights came often, and they came quickly. Sometimes it was over petty things: a glance that was a little too long, over a bunk move, a few stolen commissary items. Other times, it was survival itself that dictated violence, a quick and brutal statement that said, *I'm not the one.*

You could feel the tension in the air around B Block. It was electric, like the atmosphere before a lightning strike. As the heavy doors clanged shut behind me, I caught the eyes of the men already housed there. Some glanced up from their tables; others barely bothered to look. It didn't take long to learn that in B Block, survival meant silence and swift reaction. A car salesman's smile was a weakness. Talking too much was an invitation for violence.

Among the men there, the lifers, the gang enforcers, the ones who had tasted blood and found it familiar, I found my own rhythm that made sense in a world that did not. Here, no one pretended to be something they weren't. Masks didn't last long here; oddly enough, this place was more honest than anywhere I'd ever been before.

Looking back, I see how easy it was to start believing that anger was the only thing that could keep you safe. But at the time, there was an odd, grim pride in knowing I hadn't just survived prison life, I had carved out a place inside its darkest corner. It's a strange thing, earning your seat at a table nobody in their right mind would ever want to sit at.

For forty-five days, I lived in that limbo. I'd lie on my thin mattress, staring at the ceiling, replaying every mistake I'd ever made.

The world outside kept moving in a steady rhythm while mine froze in place. That is one of the cruelties of prison. Life carries on in full strides while you sit in a place where every day is confined to the same dull repetitive cadence. The sun rises, babies are born, seasons turn, and you stay right where you are, trapped among criminals who want to hurt you. Everyone is angry. It is not possible to describe it well.

Ellie had a baby while I was locked up. I never pretended the child was mine. She had gotten pregnant, and I knew the father was probably one of the drug dealers we both ran around with. None of it mattered to me back then. I was too far gone to care about things like paternity or responsibility. I was disappearing into my own darkness. She was disappearing into hers.

Kristy drifted in and out of my world in her own way. She always managed to get word to me through one sketchy path or another. A whisper passed through a guy on the yard, a message sent through someone who owed someone a favor, a scrap of paper with a new phone number written in purple ink. Every time I reached out, her voice felt more distant. One call to tell me Nala had died. My dog. My last living reminder of a life that once had warmth in it. Another call to tell me she was pregnant again. Another man. Another story unfolding without me.

Everything I had built on the outside dissolved while I sat in my cell. Clothes, furniture, the cars I had been proud to drive. All of it ended up scattered among the long line of men who drifted through Kristy's life while I was gone.

Those things made this sentence feel like vanishing. An erasing.

The Iowa State Department of Corrections eventually moved me to Mount Pleasant.

Mount Pleasant was a relief, to be honest. Prison life isn't easy anywhere, but it was predictable. It was a minimum-security camp, technically still prison, but compared to the concrete and razor wire fortresses I was used to, it felt like a soft landing. The air there didn't crackle with the same electric tension of maximum; it felt more like the sultry air of a summer afternoon. Men lounged in battered lawn chairs, played endless games of Spades, or shuffled to and from their jobs around the camp with a kind of indifference.

What had landed me here wasn't my reputation, which had once opened, or more accurately, *closed* doors for me all over the system. It was the nature of my charges this time: lesser, pettier things that, on paper, painted me less like a threat and more like a nuisance. A funny thing happens when your rap sheet doesn't scream *danger!* The system stops treating you like a bomb and starts treating you like a bureaucratic headache.

However, years of being wired for survival don't just unwind themselves because the fences are a little lower and the guards a little lazier. Every laugh from another prisoner felt like it had a hidden agenda; every handshake seemed a little too eager. I'd learned the hard way that the men with the easy smiles were usually the ones you had to watch the closest. But in Mount Pleasant, the violence simmered instead of boiling over; it was a place where anger fermented slowly instead of erupting unexpectedly like it had in the blocks I'd previously called home.

In maximum, the threats were immediate and obvious; here, they were subtle, clothed in fake civility and long games of patience. This demanded a different kind of toughness: less brute strength, more endurance; less making a point with your fists and more knowing when to keep your head down.

Looking back, I should have seen it coming.

At minimum security camps, the guards carry themselves with a casual arrogance that you don't often see at higher custody levels. It wasn't that they are tougher, if anything, it is the opposite. They speak to men like I was as if we are stray dogs to be herded with kicks and curses, not because they had the authority to back it up, but because they assume no prisoner would risk losing his release date over a bruised ego. Inmates at minimum security camps are closer to going home, and to most of them, a few months of swallowing their pride, taking whatever is dealt them, is a small price to pay for their upcoming freedom.

But that wasn't me. It had never been me. I didn't care if I had a week left or a lifetime; the rules I lived by didn't bend just because I was in minimum security. You come at me sideways, you're going to get all of me. All gas. No brakes.

The guard probably thought I'd roll over like the others when he barked at me in front of everyone, lacing his words with a smugness that conveyed that he didn't consider me a threat. But public disrespect was out of the question for me. By the time my mind caught up to my hands, it was already too late. I snapped. No thought-out plan, just impulsive, bone-deep rage that proved I hadn't changed a bit.

He caught every bit of my uncaged rage. Every insult, every smirk, every ounce of condescension he'd ever thrown at men like me landed back on him tenfold.

I hit him again and again, unloading all those years of weight-lifting through my fists, my thick arms driving my clenched hands deep into his head, face and body. By the time they pepper-sprayed me and dragged me off, the guard was barely conscious.

39

SOLITARY

The fallout was immediate. I was labeled a high-risk inmate again and transferred to Fort Madison, Iowa's super-max prison. There, they put me in solitary confinement, "the hole." My sentence was seven months, but it felt like seven years.

Solitary confinement is its own kind of underworld. Seven months in the hole teaches you how elastic time can be, how it stretches and warps until days smear together like wet ink. Morning does not feel like morning, night never really arrives, and the clock in your head begins to tick out of rhythm. At some point you stop counting because numbers lose their meaning.

The fluorescent lights stay on forever. They hum with a maddening buzz that crawls under your skin. After a while your body feels coated in something you cannot wash off, like a greasy film. You start wishing for darkness the way a starving man wishes for bread. A single hour without that buzzing light would have felt like a vacation, but neither silence nor darkness ever come.

People crack in there. The screams start in someone else's cell, then drift down the tier like a current that pulls at everything in its path. Some guys break their fire sprinkler heads and flood their cells just to make something happen, anything that changes the script. Water pours down through the vents above, and for a moment the monotony fractures, and the officers come running. The chaos is entertainment. Evidence of life.

Every other day, they offered me one hour of rec. When you're in solitary confinement, you're not out in the yard with other inmates during your one hour outside your cell. Instead, they bring you to these wire cages outside, small enough that you can touch every corner when you stand in the middle. Most guys take the hour just to breathe different air, but there were stretches when I was too far gone to leave my cell. My spirit had gone limp.

So I stayed in my cell and walked. Back and forth. Back and forth. The same ten steps again and again until I knew every crack in the concrete by the shape of it under my sock. You pace for so long that your thoughts do circles around your sanity. They repeat themselves. They argue.

Voices whisper lies your tired mind tries to fight off. It is agonizing. It is awful. It is a slow drip of pressure that never lets up.

There is a point where you stop talking to yourself and start listening to the silence, because even your own voice feels like a stranger. There is a point where your body is in the cell but your mind is somewhere else entirely, floating just above you, watching. Wondering if you will come back whole. Wondering if you can.

In that awful solitary stillness, something shifted.

I started talking to God.

It wasn't out of faith or devotion but desperation.

I wasn't a Christian, not yet. I hadn't surrendered, hadn't accepted Jesus. But I prayed anyway. I figured if God was real, He might listen, even to someone like me.

I didn't ask for much. Mostly, I prayed for a family. I begged God to give me a wife someday, someone who came from a good family, a family that could become mine.

And I prayed for belonging, for a place to call home. Over and over, I repeated the same plea, clinging to the hope that love could save me. I felt like an orphan, starved for connection, desperate for someone to see me as worth loving.

But deep down, I didn't believe I deserved any of it.

And I guess I didn't.

But though I didn't know it yet, heaven was already stirring, already weaving together something far beyond the hell in that cell.

Looking back, I'm grateful for those desperate prayers. They mattered. They were necessary. They came from a raw, honest place where all the pretenses had been stripped away. But at the same time, I can see now that I was still clinging to an old lie, the belief that another person could patch the gaping hole inside me. That if I could just find the right woman, every-thing broken in me would magically repair itself and make me whole. It wasn't that I had never dated good women before; I had. But good women don't heal bad wounds. The love of a woman doesn't replace the need for redemption by a Savior. And no matter how kind, beautiful, or patient a person might be, they could never fill a void that was shaped precisely to the dimensions of God Himself.

At that time, I hadn't yet realized the true nature of my hunger. I thought I was longing for a partner, for a ready-made family to graft myself into. But the truth was, I was starving for Jesus, for the restoration only He could bring. Without first letting Him fill the emptiness in my soul, I was doomed to drag every relationship down into the same pit of my neediness, selfishness, and destructiveness. Even my most personal and honest prayers, as heartfelt as they were, would have only led me back to ruin if they hadn't eventually been rerouted through the cross.

Still, I believe God honored that moment of sincerity, even knowing how imperfect my understanding was. He used it as a crack in the wall of my heart, a place where light could eventually pour in. It's humbling to realize that sometimes He answers prayers not by giving us exactly what we ask for, but by patiently reshaping our hearts so we can finally hold the blessings He always intended to give. Solitary confinement might have looked like a horrible punishment from the outside, but in that grim little box, the groundwork for real, lasting transformation was being laid.

The Bible puts it like this, "What the enemy meant for evil, God turns for good."

Those seven months in the hole were the darkest of my life. I thought I'd known suffering, but this was a new low. By the time they let me out, I was a shell of who I'd been. I was sent back to the general prison population, and I wasn't the same. I was broken, and I didn't know if I would ever be right again.

I was eventually sent back to Anamosa State Penitentiary. I had been there before, several times, in fact. The place still carried the same ancient gloom that is unique to that old, limestone prison. And it's a maximum-security prison, but it wasn't Fort Madison. Anamosa lacked that extra edge that came with the super-max designation. In Anamosa, there was just enough air between the bars to believe, if only faintly, that something in life could still change. Fights still broke out six or eight times a day, but it wasn't like Fort Madison.

I had a lot of anger, I had so much loss. I was mean. But I also had Bart. Bart, who I had come to know during my time at Mission of Hope. Bart, who had mentored me during my times out. Bart, who walked with Jesus. Bart, who sent me money that allowed me luxuries in the commissary.

And there was that library at Anamosa.

I spent my days doing what I always did when faced with too much time and too little freedom: I searched. Not for con-traband or status – not anymore – but for something deeper. Some truth, some answer. I drifted through philosophies: Buddhism, with its promises of detachment and inner peace; the pagan mythologies of the northern European gods, where valor and destiny clashed in endless twilight; stoicism, with its cold, clean insistence that only our own virtue mattered; even New Age mysticism, with its crystals and energy fields, offering vague hope that maybe the universe cared after all. Each system gave me a fleeting feeling, but none filled the hollow ache inside me. None explained to me what I was still so desperately trying to understand.

It was during these searching years that I met Tom Woodard. Tom was tall and wiry, and he carried himself with restless tension. We became friends, walking the yard day after day, our conversations meandering through theology, philosophy, and the grim realities of prison life. Tom was smart, and together we built sand castles of ideas, tearing them down and rebuilding them again as we tested each thought against our beliefs and experiences. I loved those talks. Being able to speak freely was a gift.

Sometimes, in the quieter moments of our walks, Tom would drift into darker territory. He'd talk about the guards, the systems of oppression, the ways a man might make a statement so loud no one could ignore it. I heard him, but I didn't hear him. I chalked it up to prison venting, the same way soldiers joke about fragging their commanding officers. Just talk. Just frustration. We all had our coping mechanisms.

But a few months after I paroled out, Tom's anger found its outlet. He killed two guards in an explosion of violence that shook the penal system in Iowa and made headlines. When I heard the news, it felt like the air had been punched from my lungs. Part of me still wrestles with that; a guilt that isn't rational but lingers all the same. I was his closest friend. I heard him. I walked beside him. Was there something I could have seen? Something I could have said? I don't know. Maybe I was just another mirror he practiced his rage against, testing whether anyone could see the problems in him before he unleashed them on the world.

Looking back, I realize that both Tom and I were searching for the same thing, a way to matter in a world determined to erase us. Only, when the answers failed to come, we each made different choices about how to use this life that has been given to us.

I was released in January 2020. The world had changed, but so had I.

The limp-spirited sense of defeat that had wrung the life out of me in solitary confinement was gone.

I walked out of Anamosa's prison gates with nothing but the clothes on my back and a burning anger in my chest. My prayers felt unanswered, and I left furious, ready to hit the ground running, determined to reclaim control by any means necessary.

40

TWENTY TWENTY

Who could have predicted that 2020 would be the year everything in my life changed? The world was in turmoil, but for me, it was the year I finally faced the reality of my own destruction and the possibility of redemption.

The world I stepped back into in 2020 was nothing like the one I had left behind three years earlier. It felt unrecognizable. The pandemic was in full swing. The roads were nearly empty, many businesses were closed, and people were hidden behind masks, not the burglary kind I had once been familiar with, but surgical masks to keep a microscopic enemy at bay.

The COVID-19 virus had swept across our culture, dismantling routines and tearing through lives, families, and communities. The news warned of rising numbers of cases and mounting death tolls, while hospitals overflowed, their hallways lined with the sick and dying. People stood six feet apart, desperate for toilet paper and disinfectant wipes. The fear was as contagious as the virus, and conversations in public places were clipped, and every cough in public triggered dirty stares.

Then came the fire. Not the literal kind, but the kind that spreads by way of rage and desperation, igniting cities from within. The streets filled with voices chanting the names of the fallen – George Floyd, Breonna Taylor, Ahmaud Arbery. The protests started as a plea for justice, then swelled into something primal. Cities burned, businesses were looted, and sirens screamed through the nights. It wasn't just one place, it was Minneapolis, Kenosha, Chicago, Portland. Even small towns that had never seen a protest in their history were now battlegrounds of grief and ideology.

The country was sharply split down the middle along invisible lines. Families divided, friendships dissolved, and strangers turned into enemies with a single misplaced sentence. Social media became a war zone of its own, a digital platform where people abandoned their usual filters and tore each other apart over masks, vaccines, race, politics.

And I was a newly released inmate trying to re-integrate.

It was, to say the least, a rough environment for that to happen well.

Then the sky fell.

In August, the people of Iowa were introduced to a word almost no one in the state had ever heard before: "derecho." It was an inland hurricane that roared right across Eastern Iowa, almost without warning, and it flattened everything in its path. Winds of 140 miles per hour snapped power lines, ripped roofs from homes, and turned century-old trees into splintered corpses across the streets. Cornfields, miles upon miles of healthy green crops, were smashed into the dirt. Cedar Rapids was hit especially hard, with many neighborhoods decimated. The formerly tree-filled city lost 70% of its tree canopy.

Those who had spent a lifetime assuming that disasters happened to other people were hit with a big dose of reality. The storm lasted an hour, the damage lasted months. Electricity was out in some areas for weeks. The hum of generators became the new city soundtrack. This disaster wasn't on the national news like the wildfires in California or the hurricanes on the coasts, so few outside of Iowa knew the extent of the damage. But those of us who lived through it knew.

That was 2020. A year of masked faces, burning cities, social tension, and an unexpected apocalypse.

And that was the world I had to re-enter when I left prison, already carrying the weight of my past and struggling to find my footing.

When I got out, I moved in with my mentor, Bart Woods. He had always believed in me, even when I had given up on myself. I was doing good, better than I ever had. Living in Bart's house felt like breathing clean air for the first time in my life. It was safe there. Steady. A place where men gathered around the dinner table and talked about real things, where wisdom was shared, and where demons weren't welcome.

Unfortunately, the demon of addiction is relentless. It waits in the background of an addict's existence, lurking in the shadows, and the moment you let your guard down, it attacks.

My friend Chad called.

Chad and I had become friends during the reckless years with Ellie and Kristy and methamphetamines.

I liked Chad, and we understood each other because we'd both done time.

Whereas burglary and violence – and later drugs – were what got *me* into trouble, *Chad* was a bank robber. And like me, he liked women and amphetamines. When he called, the steadiness and wisdom and safety of Bart's house all suddenly felt boring. So I took his call.

One hit, and I was back.

There was no moment of hesitation, no inner war between who I was becoming and who I had been. It was like slipping into an old jacket that still fit perfectly, and when you put it on you find a $20 bill in the pocket. It felt just like that. I was high. Within a day, I was making calls. Within two, I had fully returned to the life I swore I'd never touch again.

Driven by my relapse and the stress of the world around me, I ran away from everything good and dove headfirst back into the lifelong pattern of destruction that I'd always known.

So I called Mandy.

41

TRAP HOUSE

Mandy lived in a small house in Stanwood, Iowa, about 30 miles east of Cedar Rapids. It was just a single-story rental with weather-worn siding and a patchy front yard. I moved in, but it wasn't home.

Stanwood is a town people pass through. It has a gas station, a few bars, and a general store. The streets are empty and not especially well maintained. People get stuck in towns like this.

Mandy was the kind of girl who, in towns like this, men lose their footing around. She was equal parts invitation and warning sign, the sort of girl everyone told you to steer clear of.

I met her on a dating app, both of us pretending to be casual about the chaos we were dragging behind us. We talked for a few hours, not long enough to know anything about the other, but long enough to convince ourselves we knew enough. We met that same day. No hesitation. No second thoughts. I was fresh out of prison, hungry for something that felt like belonging. She was the first person who looked at me like I was exciting instead of broken, like my wildness was a feature instead of a flaw.

She leaned into that part of me. She liked the edge I lived on, liked the heat that came from someone who had nothing to lose. And I liked the way she was, too. It was a match neither of us should have struck, but once the spark caught, we let it burn.

She had two kids, but you wouldn't know it unless she told you. They were with her mom most of the time, which left Mandy free to do what she wanted. And what she wanted was to party, to get high, to run with the kind of people we both should have avoided, and to lose herself in the night and wake up in the afternoon.

She wasn't looking to change. And that's exactly why I went to her.

Bart's house had been safe, but it had also come with expectations like accountability and self-discipline. Bart had wisdom and knew the dangers ahead for me. And I couldn't face them, or him. I couldn't sit across the dinner table from Bart and look him in the eye, knowing all the things I had done.

But Mandy? Mandy didn't care.

Her house wasn't a home; it was a trap house with no expectations. She rented the house but barely kept up with it. It smelled like stale cigarettes and burnt foil. The carpet was stiff from filth ground into it, the couches were stained and sagging, and the kitchen sink was always piled with dishes. People came and went at all hours, eyes hollow, hands twitchy, every one of them carrying some kind of ghost on their back.

Nobody here would tell me to stop. Nobody would look at me with disappointment or remind me of who I had been trying to become.

Here, I could use without feeling any pressure to stop.

My old ways of making money (the only ways I knew) took over my life again to support my habit. But this time, I wasn't just smoking meth, I was shooting up. The moment I felt that needle in my vein, I knew I had lost control.

42

MEET MY NEMESIS

M eth is the most destructive drug on earth. It warps your mind, your body, and your soul. It isolates you until you are nothing but a shell, consumed by fear, paranoia, and desperation.

There's a point of no return when the needle slides in. The world tightens around you and shrinks to that moment, and then everything explodes outward.

The first time a person shoots up meth, some hesitation lingers as fingers shake and the pulse thrums behind the ears. The lighter crackles, the glass bubble glows orange, the vapor swirls, and then it's drawn up, thick and milky. The spoon's edges are charred, a blackened rim of past mistakes. A cotton ball soaks it up, a syringe tip grazes the surface, and the plunger draws back, pulling in the poison escape.

The tourniquet tightens – a belt or a shoelace, whatever is available. Veins pop, the skin stretches thin and pale. The needle hovers, then pierces. A sting, a push, then the eerie ease of the slide. Blood rushes back into the barrel, a swirling, ruby confirmation. The last barrier is gone.

And then it hits.

It doesn't creep in like a cigarette, doesn't roll smooth like a drink. It detonates. An electric storm floods the body, burning through muscles, shooting straight to the skull with ruthless precision.

Euphoria.

Heat spills from the chest, and limbs become weightless. A godlike clarity seizes the mind, and everything makes sense in an instant.

Heart slamming, pupils dilate and devour the iris. Hands move rapidly, touching the walls to feel them, fingertips flow over skin. Every nerve is alive, a thousand volts surging through circuits never meant to carry this kind of power.

But the high is never enough. It peaks too soon, and the crash is already lurking in the background, whispering, waiting.

The descent isn't gentle.

It's jagged, violent. The warmth curdles into sweat, the euphoria decays into paranoia. The skin crawls like it's covered with ants. The heart clenches, skips, races in unnatural rhythms. The mind turns on itself, cycling through thoughts too fast to hold. The jaw is clenched so tight the teeth might crack. The room, the world, everything is wrong.

The only way out is more.

And so it repeats. Another hit, another plunge. Veins start to scar, arms blossom with bruises, hands search for new places to inject – a foot, the neck, anywhere. The body wastes, the mind fractures, the soul – if it still exists – rots away in the chemical tide.

The needle never whispers promises. It doesn't lie. It delivers exactly what it is: a flood of synthetic lightning followed by an endless fall into darkness. There is no balance, no moderation. Only more, and then more, and then less of everything else. Less sleep. Less food. Less of the person who existed before that first injection.

The needle is a door that only opens one way.

Less than two months after that first hit, I was barely human. My body was deteriorating, my mind unraveling. At 3 a.m. on a freezing February morning, I sat on the stained, sunken-in couch of the trap house. There was no power. No heat. Who was paying bills? I couldn't remember the last time I had eaten. I had been awake for at least ten days. My thoughts were frantic, disconnected.

The darkness in the house wasn't just lack of light.

Things were very, very dark.

Desperate for something, anything, I grabbed my phone and started Googling: "If you don't believe in Jesus, are you just screwed?"

I had always wrestled with faith. I knew there was a God, I could feel it, but how could I be sure Jesus was Him? How could I know I wasn't just believing what I had been taught because I am a white guy in America? I didn't want blind faith. I wanted something real.

Google responded with empty platitudes. "Faith it till you make it!"

That answer infuriated me! Was that all there was? A blind leap in the dark? I needed something solid. Something that could save me before I disappeared completely.

Out of desperation, I called Bart. I don't know what I was expecting, but I was relieved when he answered. I certainly hoped he had a better answer to my question than Google did, whatever that might be. And maybe he could help me find a way to rekindle whatever tiny spark of life and hope might be left inside me. He told me to meet him at the café at Veritas Church in Cedar Rapids the next day.

I wasn't sure why I went; he told me to, so I did. That was all.

I showed up at the church in a stolen car.

A guy like me didn't have to try too hard to find a job as a car salesman.

I had talked my way into a Jaguar from the lot and then stopped showing up to work. They reported it as stolen.

When I parked it at the curb and stumbled into the cafe, I looked like a dying man.

My skin was pale and dirty, my eyes were hollow, and my grungy clothes hung off of me. I know I looked like a junkie, a criminal, and a lost cause … and I was all three of those.

A pastor named Richard Marsceau joined Bart and me at a table. I felt people around us staring and I knew instantly what they were thinking: I didn't belong there, in this nice, modern downtown church cafe. But Bart and Richard? They didn't see me that way. When they looked at me, it was like I mattered. Like I was worth rescuing.

They were talking to me about grace, the gospel, about Jesus.

I was so sick coming down off my high that morning that I couldn't hear them.

It was impossible to concentrate.

I hadn't slept in over a week, I was in a deep drug-addled psychosis, and I was coming down.

I got up from the table and went to the bathroom.

I had some dope in my pocket.

I took off my shoe in the church bathroom toilet stall, took off my sock, and used a vein in my foot to shoot up.

That was the only way I could be present enough to continue the conversation about saving my soul.

When I walked back to the table, I could feel my foot throbbing.

They knew. They had to know. But they didn't shame me or push me away.

They had a message to give me. And I was finally ready to hear it.

With my voice barely above a whisper, I asked, "Is it okay if I choose to believe that Jesus is God even though I can't wrap my human mind around it?"

Pastor Richard leaned forward, his eyes looking at me steadily.

"Duh, Kyle … that's what faith is."

Finally, after all the years, it landed.

I had always thought faith was something you had to feel, something you had to be completely certain of. But what if faith was a choice? What if it wasn't about having all the answers, but about making the decision to believe even when you didn't fully understand? I didn't know it then, but those questions would change my entire life.

Something inside me broke free. A flood of emotion surged through me. Moments later, Bart and Richard invited me to ask Jesus into my life. And for the first time, I did. They had the wisdom to lead me in prayer right that minute. And I prayed.

Ten days without sleep, ten days without food, ten days chasing the false euphoria that had turned into torment. I had reached the bottom.

I felt something.

Didn't hear a voice, didn't see a vision, just felt a presence.

Something big. Something beyond myself.

God.

God was the only word my shattered mind could grasp, the only thing that made sense in that pivotal moment.

I felt the weight of everything I had ever done press down on me, not as condemnation, but as truth. The truth of my brokenness, the truth of my rebellion, the truth that I had lived every second of my life pushing God away, and yet, He was still there.

I had expected judgment, expected the full force of the shame I had been drowning in for years. But instead, there was something else: love.

How unexpected.

Love so deep and consuming it made my breath catch in my throat. Love that saw me exactly as I was – in all my filth, my depravity, my selfishness – and did not turn away. Love that did not flinch at the darkness inside me but instead reached for it, as if to pull me out of the grave I had dug for myself.

I crumbled under that love. I had spent my whole life fighting against the world, against myself, against God. And in that moment, I understood what surrender was. Not defeat, not submission to some unseen force that would crush me beneath its will, but a release. The loosening of my fingers around the grip of my own destruction. The giving up of my illusion of control. The willingness to stop running and fall into the arms of the One who had been pursuing me all along.

I collapsed onto the floor, tears streaming down my grimy face. My body convulsed in exhaustion, hunger, and withdrawal. I had nothing left. I felt lighter than I ever had. For the first time in my life, I wasn't carrying my own weight. I wasn't standing on my own strength. I was finally willing to give up.

Jesus.

The name hit me like a tidal wave,. I had heard it before, dismissed it before, mocked it before. But now, it was everything. The realization came all at once: Jesus is good! Not just in some abstract, religious way. Not just in the way people in churches said He was. But in the raw, undeniable way that goodness exists at its purest form.

He was good because He had been there the whole time. He was good because He loved me despite me giving Him every reason not to. He was good because He had been inviting me while I destroyed myself instead, but He didn't leave, He didn't give up on me. He knew that I would eventually come to the end of myself.

And now, here I was, empty and broken, with absolutely nothing left to give.

And He took the weight, the pain, the past, the shame. He took my wrecked and worthless life and offered me something new. A life not built on my own schemes, whims, self-indulgence, not driven by my own selfish desires, but surrendered to Him.

Full, unadulterated surrender. It wasn't a grand gesture, not some noble declaration. It was a whisper in the wreckage. A desperate, ragged breath as I let go of myself and gave everything over to the only One who had ever truly wanted me.

Jesus, I am Yours.

And in that moment, I wasn't lost anymore. I wasn't alone. I wasn't hopeless. I was found. I was held. I was loved.

Everything changed that day. The world outside was still the same, but inside, I felt different.

Bart didn't leave me to figure it out alone. He walked with me through the brutal days that would follow. My body raged against me, demanding the poison I had been feeding it. I shook. I vomited. I begged for relief. Every second was a battle between the part of me that wanted to live and the part of me that had been willing to die. Bart was there through it all, reminding me why I was fighting.

Some nights, the ghosts of my past still tried to drag me back, but I clung to one truth: I wasn't alone anymore. God was with me.

After I turned my life over to God, I wanted the change to come all at once. I had seen it happen for other people. I had heard the testimonies where the moment of surrender snapped the chains of addiction in an instant. They walked out of the altar call and never touched the thing that ruined them again. I love those stories. I believe those stories. But that was not my story.

My road did not straighten out overnight. It curved through relapses, bad choices, destructive patterns and old shadows I thought I had already outrun.

I was an intravenous meth user whose body did not forget its cravings just because my heart cried out for grace. I felt like a fraud, telling God I wanted Him more than anything while still feeling the pull of the thing that almost killed me.

But even in the relapses, something had changed. Before God, it was just me trying to white-knuckle my way through hell. After God, even when I stumbled, I stumbled into His hands. Surrender did not make me perfect. It made me saved. It gave me a strength that was not mine, a strength that met me in the mess and carried me through it.

Little by little He pulled me forward. Every time I fell, He gave me the strength to rise. Every time the craving roared, He whispered that I was not fighting alone. It taught me how to depend on Him instead of myself.

43

THIS CONFUSING NEW LIFE

Let me get more specific.

The weeks following my decision to turn my life over to God were a whirlwind. Everything was changing at once, but nothing was settled yet.

I was still in Stanwood, living with Mandy in the trap house. I had made the commitment to turn my life around, but the environment I was in didn't reflect that commitment. I needed a change, and I needed it fast.

In my desperation, I turned to the only people I felt had the power to help me: the Christian community. I was new to faith and still grappling with the magnitude of the transformation I was seeking. I wanted to be a new person so badly. I wanted to wake up one morning with a clean heart, a clear mind, and a story that made sense again. But sickness like mine was not something I picked up overnight. It was built over years of chaos and compromise, years of running from myself. So it was never going to disappear in a single sunrise.

And it didn't.

I had been living with Bart and that was disintegrating, so he helped me find a friend to live with.

Randy lived on a farm just outside of North Liberty, the kind of place where gravel roads are slowly getting hemmed in by development. I went there hoping to lay low for a bit, to disappear into the wide Iowa night and maybe get my footing back. But Randy was dealing with his own addiction, and whatever good intentions I carried with me didn't last long.

Almost as soon as I arrived, we were drinking. Then came the cocaine. Then came something I had only tried one other time, LSD – acid. I took it casually, without ceremony, without fear. At first, nothing happened. I remember thinking it didn't work, that maybe it was weak or fake or that I was somehow immune. And then it did work. All at once.

The mix of alcohol, cocaine, and that powerful hallucinogen was too much. My mind came apart. I wasn't just confused, I was gone. I lost touch with reality in every sense of the word. I began breaking things around Randy's house: glass, doors, whatever my hands could reach. Randy was also tripping, just as lost as I was, and had no idea how to handle what was happening in front of him. Eventually, fear cut through the haze enough for him to call the police.

To me, none of it felt real. I was convinced the entire thing was a dream. When the police showed up, I still thought I was asleep on the couch, that this was all playing out in my head. I resisted them, not out of defiance, but because I genuinely believed none of it mattered. Dreams don't have consequences.

Then they released a dog.

The pain was instant and savage. The dog tore into my calf, and I remember screaming, a sound that felt like it came from somewhere other than my body. Even then, part of me thought it wasn't real. Pain, sirens, shouting, all of it blurred together as I was taken to the University of Iowa hospital.

In the ambulance, I thought the paramedic was an angel.

In the emergency room, they cut my coat off me. It was full of feathers, and as they worked on me, feathers floated through the air under the harsh hospital lights, reinforcing the idea that I was in heaven, and angel feathers were all around.

I was still tripping, still detached, watching feathers drift down like snow and thinking this whole thing was unreal, beautiful in a twisted way.

Then I saw my leg.

That was the moment the dream ended. There was a chunk of flesh missing, torn clean away. Blood, bandages, empty space where muscle should have been. I remember realizing, "Oh no. This is real! This actually happened!"

Because it was during COVID, and because nothing I had done crossed whatever invisible line they were enforcing at the time, I was released a couple hours later. No jail. No clothes. Just a thin blue-green hospital gown with my butt hanging out. I walked out into the night exposed, humiliated, and exhausted.

At around three in the morning, I hailed a cab in downtown Iowa City and gave the driver Randy's farm address. Gravel crunched under the tires when we pulled in. Terrified because I'd just torn the place up, threatened him, and got hauled off by the cops, Randy was justifiably reluctant to let me back inside.

But, maybe because he's such a nice guy, or maybe because I seemed a lot less threatening, shivering in a hospital gown outside, he let me back inside after he realized I had come down. He didn't say much. He just pointed to the couch. I collapsed onto it and slept.

Morning light tells the truth. When we woke up, the house looked like a war zone. Broken windows. The front door smashed in. Kitchen cabinets hanging loose. Picture frames shattered across the floor. We stood there, silent, surveying the damage, both of us thinking the same thing.

"Oh God. That was bad."

I wasn't allowed to stay another night. And honestly, I didn't need to be told why.

I didn't know how to go about making the change that needed to be made. I felt overwhelmed, uncertain, and isolated. So, I did something I'd never done before. I reached out on Facebook, openly asking for help.

In my post, I explained my situation as best as I could: I was in recovery, a new believer, and homeless. I needed a safe place to live and a fresh start. I wasn't sure exactly what I was asking for or even if "it" existed, but I knew I couldn't do this alone.

Within minutes, a message popped up in my inbox from a family I had never met. The Walkers.

Matt and Cindy Walker were an amazing Christian couple with three kids and a beautiful home in a suburban area near Cedar Rapids. They were strangers to me; they didn't know me, and they didn't know anyone who knew me. But somehow, they had heard clearly from God. They felt a calling they couldn't explain, but they were sure it was from God so they obeyed without hesitating. Their response felt nothing short of miraculous: They were willing to take me in. They hadn't even met me.

I showed up on their doorstep just twelve hours later with a couple of bags of belongings, everything I owned at that point. I couldn't believe it. The kindness they showed me was overwhelming. It was as if they were already family. There was no judgment, no questions about my past. They accepted me with all my brokenness and immediately loved me unconditionally.

Christ was not something they talked about only on Sundays. He was front and center in their daily life. Every night, without fail, Matt would open the Bible and read aloud while we all gathered together. We sat in the same room, kids stretched out on couches or floors, ranging in age from ten to seventeen, and no one complained or rolled their eyes. When it was Bible time, everyone just made their way to the living room and settled in, sometimes the kids before the adults. It was just what we did. Scripture was not forced, it was shared, happily and contentedly.

Dinner time at the Walkers' house was sacred too. Meals were intentional, made with care and good ingredients, evidence that someone had thought ahead. The kids helped cook, and we all sat together, prayed together, then ate together. There was laughter, conversation, the clink of forks against plates. For someone who had lived so much of life in chaos and isolation, those meals were grounding.

The house was full of life. They had animals everywhere. Dogs, cats, turtles, flying squirrels – and more cats – and then there was me, a felon, a different kind of stray added to the mix. Somehow, they let me fit right in. It was not elegant, it was safe. Safety was something my nervous system was still learning to recognize.

I loved their family traditions. One that stands out is Easter. Every year, the kids would get their swimming suits for the year tucked into our Easter baskets. I was already an adult, already carrying the weight of a long past, yet they included me without a second thought. I got a swimsuit in an Easter basket. I was one of the kids. Not in a diminishing way, not in a way that erased who I was, but in a wholesome way that let me feel that love and inclusiveness. Cindy was only a few years older than me, yet she treated me in a way that felt maternal without being patronizing. It was a strange and beautiful grace.

I was being loved, and for the first time in a long time, that love felt stable enough to hold me while God did His quiet, patient work.

The Walkers didn't push me to get my life together right away or even to contribute to the household. They didn't put any pressure on me days, weeks, or even months later to move out. I was given a safe space to heal where I could just "be." Looking back, I realize how much I needed that. I needed people who loved me, not for anything I had accomplished or might be able to do for them, but simply because I was a person in need of love.

I learned the art of the restart. One day at a time. One moment at a time. When I slipped, I learned to stand back up.

I didn't learn how to restart all at once. I learned it slowly, awkwardly, and often through failure. One day at a time. One moment at a time. Sometimes one breath at a time.

At first, I thought restarting meant fixing everything, cleaning it all up; getting it right and never slipping again. But life, and change, doesn't work like that. Healing doesn't either.

When I slipped, I didn't disappear to the bar, hiding from people who would hold me accountable, running to the people who would never hold me accountable.

So recovery started becoming about direction. Was I choosing honesty over lying, presence over panic, humility rather than shame?

One of the biggest battles was happening in my own mind. The negative dialogue ran constantly. Fear replayed the past like a courtroom tape, accusing me over and over. Anxiety was constant. I was exhausted from living everywhere except where I actually was.

Restarting meant realizing something simple and freeing: The past already happened. The future I was terrified of rarely came to pass. But the present was where life was actually unfolding, and it was the moment that I could affect. Learning to stay present changed everything. When I forced myself to stay here, right now, I had a chance.

The other part of the art of the restart that was so important was – and is – practicing gratitude, even stubborn gratitude. That shifted something inside me.

There was always something to be thankful for, even on hard days, and there still is. My "go-to gratitudes" became things like the gift of being able to breathe. Mercy. Another chance. People who didn't give up on me. Gratitude didn't erase pain, but it gave pain a smaller voice.

Worship also became an anchor in all of this. When I felt off, disconnected, or overwhelmed, worship brought me back into alignment. I believe we were created to worship God, and when we do, we step into the purpose we were designed for. For me, worship often comes through music, songs that carry truth into places words alone can't reach. Sometimes it comes through silence, sitting still before God with nothing to prove and nothing to perform.

And woven through all of the restarts was community. People showed up. Not because I had it together, but often because I didn't. Rather than pushing them away from me, I reached out to good people, Christians, who would listen. They prayed. They stayed.

The art of the restart isn't flashy. It's learning, again and again, that failing doesn't disqualify you as long as you're willing to get back up.

And in the middle of all that stumbling, people showed up. People who saw something in me I could not see in myself. They stood close when I felt unworthy and stayed steady when I shook. They loved me before I knew how to love myself, and somehow their belief carried me farther than my own strength ever could.

Little by little, through a thousand small restarts, a different man began to take shape. Not overnight, not cleanly, but honestly. And that slow, steady becoming turned out to be the real miracle.

Although I was doing better physically, my mind was still messed up by years of drug use, prison, running.

I wasn't ready for a full-time job yet, my ability to think clearly hadn't formed and I wasn't stable enough emotionally to be reliable in a job.

So in those early months of this new life, I was like a young deer trying to find his footing, a fawn on shaky legs, vulnerable. It probably looked exactly like that when I was at my best, and then it probably looked like I was the same loud, destructive, bombastic character seeking adrenaline and dopamine and attention. It goes like that.

It wasn't as if my mania had somehow resolved itself when I accepted Jesus, it wasn't as if extreme highs and lows were behind me, and it wasn't as if I suddenly had long attention spans.

But I was making progress. I did odd jobs here and there, things that didn't require much mental effort but that gave me some purpose and a little bit of self-confidence. The Walkers never once complained or seemed disappointed in me. They just loved me, and I felt it.

As the months passed, I began to heal, slowly but surely. The Walkers had provided the stability I needed, and their love and support allowed me to start building a life for myself. I met some folks, the Wasson family, who let me use a shop on their property for a handyman business. It was amazing – they had a huge metal building that I never could have afforded, and it was mine to use. I worked at my own pace, figuring things out as I went along, and as time passed, I felt stronger emotionally, physically and spiritually.

But in the midst of this healing and support, my struggles weren't over. I wasn't immune to relapse.

I was drunk at a bar waiting for my dealer when the door creaked open behind me. I didn't even bother turning around. A moment later, I felt someone sit beside me. I looked up, expecting chaos. Instead, it was Bart. Not a word. Just presence. His silence was louder than any sermon ever preached.

Years earlier, I'd asked Bart to become my mentor. But what he became was my ally.

Not mentor. Not coach. Not counselor. Ally. A word that means being a steady hand of support. An ally stays when it's hard, listens when it's awkward, loves when it's undeserved.

Sitting on that stool I realized what it was to have an ally. When I was homeless, living at Mission of Hope, Bart didn't just hand me a Bible tract and walk away. He and his wife have let me live with them more than once. He helped me get my driver's license back when I didn't even believe I deserved one. We still talk every single week, without fail. He's sat with me in the darkest places, not to fix me, but to be with me.

Bart didn't rescue me from that bar. He sat with me until I learned how to stand. He didn't demand I change. He believed I could, and he lived in a way that made me believe it too. He was my ally when I didn't even know what that meant.

I could have gotten sober sooner if only I'd seen that alcohol was my problem.

I hated being drunk, but I liked drinking.

I could go to the bars, have a few drinks, and be okay. But inevitably some girl would wonder if I could help find cocaine, and I could, and once I had a few drinks in me, it opened the door to a relapse.

I thought alcohol was my only problem, but I wish that I'd made the connection sooner that alcohol led to drugs.

I lived with the Walkers for almost a year.

A small local ministry called Hope CDA was growing.

Bart introduced me to the executive director, Ron Ziegler. Hope CDA is a program designed to help men who were living on the streets or recently out of prison. It wasn't well-known in the community, and the structure wasn't fully developed. Ron is a humble, passionate man of God with phenomenal leadership experience and skills.

Ron saw potential in me, and he offered me the position of Development Director. He also let me move into one of the program houses to provide some leadership and stability for the men in the program.

In all honesty, I wasn't the right person for that role at the time; I should have been *in* the program. I wasn't emotionally stable, and I still had so much more healing to do. But I took the position and, looking back, I realize it was God's grace that allowed me to be there. I wasn't qualified but, fortunately, God loves to use unqualified people.

Under Ron's leadership, the program grew in participants, volunteers, staff, funding, and success stories of transformed lives. I learned more than I could have ever imagined about fundraising, leadership, accountability, trust, and conducting myself in a professional environment.

But Ron gave me something I really needed: The freedom to fail. Without that space to make mistakes, I wouldn't have been able to grow in my role or as a person.

And I made my share of mistakes.

At times I could be erratic, I could deal harshly with the men in the program, I got myself involved in crazy situations …

and I relapsed. In a program designed for stability where I was intended to be one of the leaders, I allowed myself to be seduced by my demons.

I remember a time that I was giving a guy a drug test. He tested dirty. I was all over him, "When are you going to figure this out!? When are you going to get out of this cycle!?" As I yelled at him across the desk, the truth was that I had done cocaine off that very desk a couple of days earlier – I would have also tested dirty at that exact moment.

I couldn't comprehend my own hypocrisy.

As the program grew, I connected with a number of amazing men, participants in the program, who would become key people in my journey. We were all struggling, all working through our own issues, but we had one another for support, encouragement, and accountability. I connected with a band of brothers who understood my past and accepted me as I was. And that made all the difference.

We would call and text one another to see how the other was doing. We knew "the signs" that someone was struggling and we could, and did, call one another out. We'd all struggled with addiction, we'd all been incarcerated, and we'd all made a new commitment to Jesus, which created a bond as we all fought our way through our pasts and toward brighter futures.

The first time I heard the word honor, it felt like an echo
from some ancient world, like the clang of steel on a battlefield
or the whispered vows of knights who swore their lives to
something greater than themselves.

It is not a word we use much anymore, not in a world that prizes
comfort over sacrifice. But I came to realize honor is not a relic.
It is alive. It walks on two feet. It looks you in the eye.

Honor is quiet, and at first you might not notice it. I didn't.

It does not wave a flag or demand attention.
It shows itself in the steady way a man carries himself,
in how he listens more than he speaks, in how he shoulders
responsibility without complaint.

It came to me, personally, in the way one man trusted me when
I was fresh out of prison. Most would have turned me away.
I worked for him, stumbled under his leadership, and yet was
given the space to try again.

He never called it honor, never preached it, never
self-proclaimed it. But the word became the way I knew him.
How I describe him in my mind.

My wife said it once, in passing: "He is an honorable man."

And from that day forward, I began to see it everywhere in him,
how he spoke truth without cruelty, how he stayed steady when
nothing else was, how he gave grace without
lowering the standard.

Honor, I learned, is not the same as love, but it is close. Love is
felt in the heart, but honor is chosen in the will. Honor protects,
it builds … it is respect in action.

That is what I saw lived out, day after day, by the man
I worked under – Ron.

His strength was not self-made. It was built up through a long walk with Jesus, the kind of faith that hones a soul until it shines without trying. From that place came his patience, his steadiness, his depth. To be around him was to be reminded that life is not about climbing higher, but about standing truer.

I think honor could really be about recognizing the Spirit's work in others. It is treating people not only as they are, but as who they are becoming. That is what Ron did for me. He honored me long before I knew how to live honorably myself.

Looking back, that was helping me grow.
I couldn't see it then, but I can now.

When I think of him now, I picture a lighthouse on a dark storm-battered coast. It does not move. It does not shout. It simply shines in the night. The waves may rise and fall, the ships may be battered upon them, but the light remains, dependably, steadily pointing out danger, and helping you find your way home.

And so I circle back: Honor is not gone. It's not common, but it has not faded into history. It is alive, and I know – because I sailed out of a long dark night, guided by its light.

"Humility is the fear of the Lord;
its wages are riches and honor and life."

Proverbs 22:4

In June of 2020, just four months after I had turned my life over to God, Andrea Wasson introduced me to Dawn. Dawn was everything I had prayed for when I was in prison. She was stunningly beautiful and exceedingly kind, but most importantly, she loved Jesus. Although she worked for a local ministry, she lived an hour's drive north of me in a home she owned. She came from a good, stable Iowa farming family. And she herself was stable emotionally, financially, and spiritually. Everything I had dreamed of when I was praying for a wife from my cell in solitary confinement in Fort Madison prison seemed to be in front of me in the person of Dawn.

Prior to our second date, I called Dawn to reveal to her who I really was. I wanted to be completely honest with her, and I needed to know if she could accept me for who I was. I spent hours on the phone with her, telling her every dark detail of my past. I felt like she had the right to know the good, the bad, and the very ugly. After sharing my worst secrets, worst habits, and worst crimes and offenses, I asked her what she thought of all the terrible things I had done.

After a pause of a few seconds she responded, "I like steak."

She was still interested! And there would be steak on our next date.

That date was going to be at a fancy steakhouse on the river in Independence, near where Dawn lived. As I drove the hour north to see her, a terrible storm developed. The rain was coming down in torrents, blinding me, and the wind was fierce, nearly blowing the car off the road. I began to doubt whether I should continue. I almost turned around, but something in me made me press on. Finally the storm began to let up, and the closer I got to Dawn's house, the more the storm cleared. By the time I arrived, the road was bone dry, birds were chirping, and everything felt calm. It was as though God was sending me a message, telling me to keep going, to press on with this relationship. I took it as a sign.

Time quietly slipped out of the room without saying goodbye. Somewhere between laughter and long pauses, between stories and shared silence, it settled into my chest with a calm certainty, I was falling in love with her.

Over the next few months, we hated being apart. We found every excuse to see each other, rearranging schedules, stealing time, stretching evenings longer than they should have been. Dating Dawn was unlike anything I had known before. She was beautiful and educated, but what set her apart is that she loved Jesus with a sincerity that was lived, not performed. She worked for a ministry, putting her convictions into action through her work. Dawn carried that gentle, free-spirited, Jesus-hippie kind of faith that felt both pure and wild. I was drawn to it, to her. She loved the farm life, the simplicity and the work. Her family owned a farm, and she had grown up with dirt under her nails and responsibility in her bones.

Our dates were simple and full. Little restaurants and quiet cafés became our favorites, so different than the dirty bars and noisy nightclubs I'd known. Sometimes we would drive back to the small town she lived in, wandering antique shops, lingering over old things with stories etched into their edges. We worshiped together in the car, windows down, music turned up, our voices off key but honest. We worshiped at events scattered across the city, shoulder to shoulder with strangers who felt, for a moment, like family.

I was new to faith, still learning how to walk in it without tripping over my own feet. Dawn, on the other hand, was deeply rooted in the Christian community. She knew the language, the rhythms, the seasons of belief. Being near her made me want to grow, to be better, to heal. It felt like things were finally lining up, like life was offering me something good and wholesome.

But even as everything seemed to be falling into place, there was an undercurrent I could feel but had not yet named. Beneath the joy and the closeness, there were still unresolved issues inside me, spiritual attachments and generational weight I had never fully faced. Old wounds, old patterns, things passed down to me and things I'd picked up along the way. I had not dealt with them yet, and though I did not fully understand how or why, they were already reaching into our relationship, setting the stage for a testing that was coming.

44

BRIDE & GROOM

Dawn and I were married on June 11, 2021, in a beautiful ceremony in a rustic barn near her home. As her family surrounded us under the open sky, the summer sunbathed everything in golden light. Hundreds of people were there, people who loved Dawn deeply, people who had watched her grow up, people who shared the same bloodline and carried the same history. But I wasn't related to any of them.

That truth weighed heavily on me. I had a wife, a partner for life, but standing there on my wedding day, surrounded by her family and their love for each other, I didn't feel like I was being adopted, I felt like an outsider. That feeling fed the orphan spirit that had haunted me my whole life.

I didn't know it then, but I'd come to understand that this "orphan spirit" is something like a heart posture shaped by fear, insecurity, and separation rather than by the assurance of being a loved child of God. It is not, of course, a clinical diagnosis, but I had those too.

Jesus speaks directly to this idea in John 14:18 when He says, "I will not leave you as orphans; I will come to you," affirming that God's intention is closeness, not abandonment.

But the orphan spirit isn't just conceptual, I'd come to learn, it's an actual spirit, an agent of the kingdom of darkness, that attaches to us when we are in the kinds of trauma that I had been in. Spiritual warfare as described in the Bible is real, and without knowing it, I'd been battling it all my life.

In that first year of our marriage, everything was amplified, intense. The highs were bright enough to make us believe anything was possible, and the lows were dark enough to make us wonder if we would ever find our footing. We were newly married and still learning the rhythm of each other as newlyweds do. But Dawn had come from a very different background, and my past wasn't fully behind me.

There were sweet mornings when we moved around the kitchen like we had been together for decades, little victories that felt like signs from heaven that we were going to make it. There were nights when we held each other and talked about our future with a hope that made us feel brave.

Mixed into all of that were the darker chapters. I relapsed several times and every one of those nights felt like a trap-door opening beneath us. The months of sobriety that I did hold onto gave us both something to cling to. They were real months, healthy months. Months when I showed up for her and for Hope CDA. Months when I was clear minded enough to dream again. Those stretches gave her just enough reason to believe that the man she married was still in there fighting to surface. And she fought alongside me, fought for me, to a degree that I think few people would have or could have. I know it was not easy for her.

We got a house, a Hope CDA House, one of the homes in Cedar Rapid's inner core that had been purchased and rebuilt by the men in the program. We came to know some of the neighbors, and some became important friends, people like Travis Kolder and Austin and Jenny Chadima. These people were living in an inner-city neighborhood "on purpose" and that felt like the right move for us, too.

In 2021, when the world was still buried under the weight of COVID, it was easy to hide behind masks and isolation and that strange time. I used all of that as camouflage. I slipped, and she felt it. I pulled away, and she felt that too. There were seasons when our home felt like two separate worlds under one roof. We had moments of deep closeness when we breathed in sync and then sudden separations when it felt like our hearts were standing on opposite shores calling out across a dark stretch of water.

Setting aside the metaphors, I didn't know how to deal with my emotions or the challenges of everyday life. I grew up in prison. I could explode in anger over anything. I would break things. I would throw temper tantrums over silly things. I would become defiant. And then I would be sweet, kind.

Manic.

I would be desperate for her love and then act as if she wasn't loving me.

I would be self-righteous and indignant despite my own crazy, toxic, volatile, destructive behavior, blaming her, gaslighting her, making myself the victim and her the problem, which couldn't have been further from the truth.

Looking back, I still do not know why she stayed. She had every reason not to. There were voices around her urging her to walk away, people reminding her that no one would blame her for choosing an easier life without me. But she stayed. She stayed when it was confusing. She stayed when it was painful. She stayed when I gave her almost nothing to work with except the occasional glimpse of who I wanted to be.

Her love in that first year was not soft or sentimental. It was stubborn. Steady in a way that still humbles me. And that year, with all its victories and all its losses, became the ground God used to begin remaking both of us.

Thank God for people like Kevin Knox, Travis Kolder, Betty Criddle, Jenny and Austin Chadima, Sam Assoey, Teeg Stouffer, Lavonne Johnson. Without a community of Christ-following friends around us, I don't know how Dawn and I ever could have made it. They showed up in our kitchen when we were at our wit's end. They took our calls at 2 a.m. They put me up in a hotel room when we needed separation. They talked me off so many cliffs. They prayed with us. They were a voice of reason – and a voice of God.

A year into our marriage, our lives changed forever when we welcomed a beautiful baby girl into the world. Eve was perfect in every way – tiny, fragile, vibrant. The first time I held her, I felt a love I had never known. It should have been enough to keep me on the right path. I told myself it would be. I had a second chance at fatherhood, and I wanted to be the father she deserved, and the husband Dawn deserved. But my demons had their claws deep in me, and no matter how much I fought, I couldn't seem to get away from them.

Several months before Eve was born, I had a significant relapse. Throughout my life, my addictions had always been cyclical: periods of sobriety eventually followed by a relapse.

Like so much of my life, I was always a binge and purge type guy. All in on something.

Relapses like this aren't like, "I did meth once."

They're like, "I got high and then had to stay high day after day."

So unfortunately, that pattern of addiction continued after Dawn and I were married, after that monumental day when I committed my life to Jesus in the church cafe.

Following God, I would learn, wasn't about being without sin, but it was about being on the right path, with Him, and learning how to live differently day by day.

So, the times of sobriety gave Dawn hope, but they would be followed by deep crashes that shattered that hope. If I wasn't high, I was drunk and partying all night, chasing the chaos of self-destruction. I'd string together a few months of sobriety, just enough for Dawn to believe in me again. But it wouldn't seem to last.

I blamed her.

I told her, and I truly believed, that if she just loved me more, I could get through this. If she could be more understanding, if she didn't push me away when I was spiraling, if she supported me better, then maybe I wouldn't have to use. I put that weight, the unbearable burden of my brokenness, on her shoulders. And she tried to love me "enough." She really tried. But it was never enough because the truth was, this wasn't about her. It was about me. I had demonic attachments.

Let me pause here, because I know that many readers are going to be coming into this part of the conversation with different theologies. Maybe you are not a Christian, or maybe you are a Christian who believes that people who commit their lives to Jesus cannot have any kind of demonic oppression.

This is a broad, difficult, and deep topic that I am not qualified to write on. I'll leave that to the theologians or – who knows – maybe a future book.

But let me explain to you in a few sentences the reality that I came to understand.

The same miracle-working God of the Bible is alive today, still working miracles.

Heaven is real. Hell is real. God is real, and we can be in a real, two-way, amazing relationship with Him through His son, Jesus Christ. God loves us, loves you, and wants you to be free, fully free, and He sent Jesus to make that possible. But it is also true that there is a real enemy whose evil minions – demons – will both torment us and use us to torment others. That classic cartoon with an angel on one shoulder and a devil on the other whispering in someone's ear? That's not too far from the truth. And as it was for me, the demons of addiction, of orphanhood, and so many others had not been broken off of me. Many people give their life to Christ and then struggle with sin, and it's not because Jesus is not enough, He is, it's that there are still demonic attachments that must be broken off, and they can be.

Mine had not been.

Some of that was my own doing, and some of it was a sickness, and some of it was spiritual, and I didn't understand any of it.

Even after surrendering to God, even after knowing – truly knowing – that I was saved, that grace covered me, and that if I died, I'd open my eyes up in heaven, something still clung to me deep inside.

I had been freed, yet I was still bound. Not possessed, oppressed. There's a difference.

I had everything I had prayed for, but it was like I was being compelled beyond my own will to do things that would once again destroy everything I'd been given. The sins I had repented of with my mouth but couldn't seem to repent of in my actions tormented me. I would stand in church, hands lifted, singing the words of deliverance, but inside, there was still a war raging.

Living in it felt impossible some days.

I would cry out to God, "Please, God, either fix me or kill me!"

I felt like a fraud. Like a man wearing clean clothes over a dirty body, smiling and nodding at all the right moments but inwardly screaming for release from the torment. I felt broken in a way even God couldn't fix.

But I knew better than that feeling. People like Bart, and Betty, people like my pastor, the Walkers, and other Christian friends who had come into my life helped me know the truth, what the Bible actually says, even when I didn't feel it.

And so I kept going, because I believed what they said, what the Bible said, even more than what I was feeling and experiencing.

I wasn't who I had been. But I wasn't yet who I was meant to be.

Kyle Orth was dying and Kyle Hunter was being born.

So I pressed forward, stumbling and weary, but still moving. Because even when I didn't feel free, I clung to the only thing I knew for certain: God wasn't finished with me yet. He was raising a new life in me.

The ups and downs of my addiction and behavior took a toll on Dawn. We almost gave up on our marriage more times than I care to remember. Sometimes she would leave. Other times, I would storm out, spending nights in a hotel, drowning in self-pity and poison from a bottle. Her family had shown up with a moving truck, ready to take her and our daughter away. They were tired of watching her suffer for a man who couldn't get it together. It was an endless cycle of destructive living.

The U-Haul pulled up like a judge handing down a verdict.

Dawn's family followed behind it, easing to the curb in front of our place. The street was loud, distant sirens, someone yelling a few houses down, a car with too much bass rattling past. The neighborhood didn't slow down just because our world was about to crack open.

Boxes waited inside. Blankets were folded. Everything felt staged, like the decision had already been made and we were just acting out the final scene.

And then Lavonne showed up.

Of all days. Of all moments. She showed up in the final hour.

Lavonne was a retired drug treatment counselor who spent her days volunteering at Hope CDA, sitting across from men who carried their lives in pieces. For a season, I had met her in her garage, sitting on folding chairs, trying to make sense of myself, trying to figure out how to stop repeating the same patterns that kept hurting the people I loved. She knew my history. She knew my blind spots. She knew how close I lived to the edge.

And somehow, she was free that day.

Divine intervention.

She walked into the house calmly, without urgency or judgment. She didn't pick sides. She didn't raise her voice. She just took in the tension, the silence, the grief hanging between Dawn and me. Then she said something that felt almost too simple for a moment this big.

She asked Dawn and me to take a walk.

Just around the block.

She told Dawn, "If you still feel the same when you get back, I'll help you pack."

No pressure. No threats. No begging. Just space.

So we walked.

Side by side. Past cracked sidewalks, chain link fences, porches with people watching the day unfold. The neighborhood kept breathing around us, kids riding bikes, someone sitting on a stoop, life happening, unaware of ours falling apart. Somewhere along that walk, the noise in my head softened. Fear loosened its grip. The story I had been telling myself, that this was already over, started to lose its power.

We talked. Slowly. Honestly. Not fixing everything. Not erasing the past. Just telling the truth in that moment.

When we turned back toward the house, I didn't know what Dawn would decide. I only knew something had shifted. The walk had slowed time. It created a pause where there hadn't been one before.

When we stepped back inside, Dawn made her choice.

She stayed.

The boxes didn't move. The U-Haul left, empty. Lavonne never had to pack a thing. And somehow, against all odds, our marriage survived another day.

To be clear: Our marriage wasn't healed. Just still standing. We were still together. God and Lavonne and Dawn gave us one more day to try again.

Then, in October of 2022, it all came to a head again.

I was ready to quit – on my marriage, on my family, on myself. I had convinced myself that God had given up on me. And if God was done with me, what was the point of fighting anymore? I decided to go back to the streets. I would give in to my addiction and let it consume me whole. Dawn and I were both done.

That night, we sat in the living room of our home on Washington Avenue, exhausted and empty. I was high. I had lost my job at Hope CDA. We had fought, we had cried, we had laid everything out, and the only conclusion we could come to was that it was over. We agreed: This was the end. Decision made.

But something buried deep beneath the layers of pain, something untouched by the drugs, the alcohol, the darkness, something whispered one last plea. Even in my high, drug-induced state, I turned to Dawn and said, "Let's give it one more night. Just one more night. If God has anything left for us, He can show us. If nothing changes by morning, we'll be done."

She was exhausted, but she agreed.

She went to bed, and I stayed awake, pacing, my heart heavy.

And then, something happened that I still struggle to put into words.

The Holy Spirit entered our house. Not in a metaphorical way. Not in a gentle, whispering presence. It was intense, undeniable power. Our house shook – literally shook – as if something unseen was tearing through it. I paced from room to room, unable to stop moving, as I watched the world around me shake.

It wasn't a hallucination. It wasn't a bad trip. It was some kind of miraculous event from the wonder-working God of Heaven and earth. The walls, the furniture, the very foundation of our home looked to me as if it were rotting before my eyes, breaking apart, disintegrating into nothing. It was as if the veil between this physical world and the spiritual world beyond it had been torn away, and I was seeing everything as it truly was, the physical and the spiritual at once.

I saw visions. I saw my past, my future, the destruction that would come if I didn't break free. I felt something touch me, something Holy, something powerful. I wept, I prayed, I screamed. I was at war with something I couldn't see, something that had held me captive my entire life.

And at the very same time, upstairs in our bedroom, Dawn was experiencing the same thing. The same presence, the same shaking, the same overwhelming power. She came downstairs hours later and when she saw me – disheveled, broken, undone – she knew.

"I'm not ready to give up," she said.

Neither was I.

It wasn't like we fell into one another's arms. We felt completely depleted. But we both knew we'd experienced something powerful, supernatural, probably the Holy Spirit, and we both had the same question, "If God is saying He will provide the answer, what's the answer? What next?"

We needed help. We needed something stronger than our willpower, which had failed us. We needed something greater than therapy, which we had tried, and which hadn't been enough. I'd been through rehab, and here I was – still addicted.

We needed deliverance.

One of the Christians who had come to walk alongside us was a friend who I met through Hope CDA. Ron had introduced us; he was a volunteer at Hope, a filmmaker who was helping make fundraising videos that could help tell the Hope CDA story.

I reached out to him and explained what was going on. When I told him what had happened, he didn't seem shocked. Instead, he responded with one word: "Deliverance."

He explained it to me, how it worked, what it would mean. At first I was hesitant. It sounded weird. But what Dawn and I had experienced the night before was weird, and I'd done so many weird things. But also: dealing with demons sounded terrifying. But I was desperate. So I said yes.

We set a date for a week later. I counted down the days with a mix of anxiety and anticipation. I didn't know what was coming, but I knew it would change everything.

And I was right.

45

NEW LIFE

I was ready to kill Kyle Orth. Not in the literal sense, though at times I wondered if it would've been easier that way, but in the sense that is born out of scriptures like these:

2 Corinthians 5:17 (NIV) "Therefore, if anyone is in Christ, *the new creation has come*: The old has gone, the new is here!"

Romans 6:6–7 (NIV) "For we know that our *old self was crucified with him* so that the body ruled by sin might be done away with, that we should no longer be slaves to sin."

Romans 6:11 (NIV) "In the same way, count yourselves *dead to sin but alive to God in Christ Jesus.*"

1 Peter 2:24 (NIV) "He himself bore our sins in his body on the cross, so that we might *die to sins and live for righteousness.*"

It wasn't that I could kill Kyle Orth, but it was that God could, if I would cooperate.

At long last, I was ready to cooperate. A new level of surrender.

If Jesus would kill Kyle Orth, I was willing to pick up my shovel and dig the grave. I would be the one to bury the identity that caused the wreckage of my life for so long.

Deliverance is a powerful thing. We barely talk about it in the Western church. Some charismatic circles do, kind of, but it's not very well understood. For all the teachings on grace and salvation and Christian living and repentance and evangelism, there are very very few on deliverance.

If my life is an example, that should change.

When I turned my life over to God in 2020, I fully believe that if I had died that day, I would have gone to heaven. I was saved. I had accepted Christ. But walking in full spiritual freedom? That was something else entirely. The chains I carried weren't just the ones I could see – addiction, orphanhood, abuse and crime.

But a person sure could see the effects on me, and on everyone around me.

I still had these spiritual attachments. Some might call them strongholds. I don't pretend to know everything, but from what I've seen, they fall into two main categories: generational curses and demonic attachments. I had both. My biggest ones were the spirit of orphanhood and the spirit of addiction.

There were others, I'm sure, but those two had their claws so deep in me that I didn't know where they ended and I began. Orphanhood is the feeling of abandonment, of being unwanted, of never truly belonging. Addiction, of course, is the restless, relentless need for something, anything, to dull the pain, to fill the void. Both had been with me for as long as I could remember. Both had dictated my life like a cruel master, shaping me into someone I didn't want to be.

Rehab, discipline, therapy, church played a role in my healing, but nothing ever got to the root of it. Nothing ever truly severed the ties. I always seemed to be fighting battles I didn't understand, losing ground I didn't even know I needed to defend.

Then came the day of my deliverance.

The man who led it was kind and thoughtful. He wasn't some showman looking to put on a performance; he was a servant of God, fully surrendered and willing to stand in the gap for others. Five people gathered around Dawn and me that day, praying, reading scripture, standing as intercessors. They had fasted beforehand, made sure their hearts were clean before God, prepared themselves for the battle they were about to step into on my behalf.

It lasted about two hours. Two hours of prayer, reading scripture, silence, and intercession. Two hours of asking, listening, commanding, and surrendering. They continued to pray until they saw nothing left.

And if I'm being completely honest? It felt anticlimactic.

I had expected something dramatic. Something out of a movie. I thought maybe I'd levitate, or that my head would spin around. Maybe I'd feel something rush out of me like a gust of wind, or maybe I'd collapse under the weight of it all. But none of that happened.

Nothing even felt different at first.

But something powerful had shifted.

The days that followed were rough. Harder than I had anticipated. Things actually got worse before they got better. It was like the spiritual world pushed back, angry that I had dared to sever ties. The attacks came as little whispers of doubt at first, old temptations knocking at the door to see if I'd let them in.

One night, I did.

And something crazy happened: It had no appeal to me.

With the demons gone, what had once been so attractive wasn't any more.

It was repulsive.

So successful days stretched into clean weeks, and things started to change.

I began to see the world differently.

The things that once had a grip on me had lost their power.

Deliverance didn't mean I was suddenly perfect, but what it did was bring me back to zero. I had been so far in the negative, operating from such a deep deficit, that I never stood a chance before. Every step I had taken up until that point felt like trying to climb out of quicksand, getting pulled back under no matter how hard I fought. Deliverance changed that. It didn't catapult me forward, it just set me on level ground for the first time in my life.

That was all I needed.

For the first time, I had a fighting chance.

Dawn saw it too. The way my reactions changed, the way old habits lost their appeal, the way I stood a little taller, spoke with more clarity.

Something else had happened too. I experienced healing.

Over the couple of years since my release from prison in 2020 I had been trying to get my mood stable and my ADHD and bipolar disorder under control with actual, legitimate, doctor-prescribed antidepressants. Among other drugs, I was prescribed a high dose of lithium – so much that it required weekly testing to make sure my liver was functioning properly. I hated being on it because it made me feel so lethargic that I couldn't lift my arms, like I weighed a thousand pounds and couldn't get out of bed.

Then – that deliverance ministry – and … I don't know. Something changed.

Suddenly my mania just fell off a cliff. Those very high highs and very low lows that flipped back and forth throughout every day; my constantly fleeting attention span, it just – regulated.

I experienced a miraculous healing from God.

It's *most honest* to say that I experienced "a significant measure" of healing, because it wasn't as if I was suddenly the most rock-steady unflappable person you'd ever met, or like my attention span went from *none at all* to *the best there is*, but it's absolutely true to say that I went from barely functional to what I think most people would agree is a normal range of human emotion.

God is deliverer, and healer too. I'm living proof.

Over the next few months, I started to understand what true freedom in Christ looked like. It wasn't about pretending I had it all together. It wasn't about being perfect. It was about knowing that the chains were broken, that I was no longer bound by things I couldn't name. It was about learning to walk as a son instead of an orphan, as a free man instead of an addict.

It was about learning to live in the identity that God had always intended for me.

Kyle Orth had to die. The old me, the me that had been shaped by pain and survival, had to be put to death. And in his place, someone new was growing.

Someone redeemed.

Someone whole.

Someone free.

Me.

They say only 2% of people who ever touch meth recover.

I don't know if that number is true, but if it's close,
if you try it once, you're stepping onto a road from
which very few will ever return.

I've seen the "2%" tattooed on people in recovery
but also on people still deep in addiction.

People I used with.

Strung out, pale, chewing their cheeks raw.

So maybe it's not scientifically accurate.

But in my experience?

It feels generous.

Here's the thing: I'm one of the 2%.

Somehow.

By the grace of God and the love of people
who refused to give up on me.

I clawed through relapses, detoxes, jail cells.

Buried people I loved.

Lost years.

Burned bridges.

But Jesus met me in the darkness.

Now? I see the 2% not as a boast, but a burden.

Because behind that number are real people.

If that number is even close, we've got work to do.

Maybe we can raise it to 3% or 4% or ... who knows?

Maybe your story is the spark someone else needs.

You are not alone. I know the shame. The whispers.

The feeling of giving up on yourself.

But Jesus hasn't given up.

He sees it all and still says, "Come home."

I love you. Even if we've never met.

Because I've been you. And I believe in you.

Let's fight together. For the 2%. The 98%. For all of us.

46

HE WHO THE SON SETS FREE IS FREE INDEED

About deliverance.

As you know by now, I definitely didn't go to seminary. I can't work out the systematic theology that creates the unassailable case for this form of ministry. But I can see deliverance in the Bible, I can see it in the ministry of Jesus, and I *have* been through it. I've been bound by the chains. I've felt the cold breath of evil inside of me. And I've also seen the chains break – snapped like brittle straw under the authority of Jesus.

So this isn't a manual or a set of step-by-step instructions. There are people far smarter than I am who've spent their lives digging into the theology, the linguistics, and the history. You should read their writings. You *should* prepare. But if you've made it this far into this book, then maybe what you're really looking for isn't a checklist. Maybe what you need is a flashlight to guide you through your own fog. A witness. A brother in the trenches saying, *"I've been there too. Let me tell you what I've seen, and how I got out."*

Deliverance is not a magic spell. It's not a chant or a command that strong-arms demons into obedience. It's not a show.

It's not a badge of spiritual superiority or some spooky rite reserved for elite Christians.

It's also not something to play around with, and it's definitely not something to fake.

At its core, deliverance is a rescue mission: Jesus coming to reclaim what's already His. And like any rescue, there are a few things that matter deeply.

First, you've got to be His. I mean really. If someone isn't saved, if they haven't surrendered their life to Jesus, then deliverance is like boarding up the windows while leaving the front door wide open. Jesus Himself warned us about this. In Matthew 12:43-45, He says,

"When an impure spirit comes out of a person, it goes through arid places seeking rest and does not find it. Then it says, 'I will return to the house I left.' When it arrives, it finds the house unoccupied, swept clean and put in order. Then it goes and takes with it seven other spirits more wicked than itself, and they go in and live there."

Without the indwelling of the Holy Spirit, the house just gets repossessed. The enemy doesn't mind being kicked out, he wants to come back with reinforcements. So salvation isn't a suggestion; it's the foundation. Without it, deliverance can do more harm than good.

And if you're married? You're one flesh. It's covenant. Genesis 2:24 says, *"...and the two shall become one flesh."* That means if there's spiritual junk tormenting one of you, it's touching both of you. It'd be like trying to mop the floor while a kid with muddy feet runs around the house. If you're yoked in marriage, you have to do this together.

Then there's the sobriety piece. I'm not saying God can't reach into the fog of addiction and set someone free, He absolutely can! I've seen Him do it! But when your mind is clear and your body is sober, you're more able to engage in the process. You're more able to stand your ground and recognize what's happening. Demons love confusion. They hide in the haze. So be sober. Not because it makes you worthy, but because it makes you *ready.*

None of that matters if the person doesn't *want* to be healed.

Let that sink in.

I've sat across from people who were tormented, writhing, hurting, angry at God, angry at the world, but when you look in their eyes, you see it: They don't *really* want to let it go. Sometimes we carry our chains like old trophies. The demon becomes our friend, a constant companion. A bad friend, but a friend nonetheless. Sometimes the pain becomes our identity. In all those cases, the devil doesn't have to fight us, we do his work for him.

That's why the question Jesus asked the man at the pool of Bethesda in John 5:6 is so important: *"Do you want to be made well?"* He wasn't being cruel. He was being *honest.* Healing takes our participation. Maybe Jesus could've healed that man without a word, but He invited him into it. When the man said yes, Jesus said, *"Take up your mat and walk."* That's what deliverance requires, its Jesus offering healing, but it's also you choosing to accept it.

Deliverance isn't just about the one being set free, it's also about the people standing in the gap.

If you're going to help someone through deliverance, you'd better be clean yourself. Not perfect. Just *repentant.* You don't walk onto a battlefield in flip-flops with sin in your backpack. Before you even think about engaging the enemy on someone else's behalf, make sure you've surrendered your own hidden places. Fast. Pray. Ask God to search you. King David said it best: *"Create in me a clean heart, O God, and renew a right spirit within me."* (Psalm 51:10)

And don't do it alone. There should be intercessors – trusted people who are praying and fasting behind the scenes. Deliverance isn't a one-man show; it's a team effort. There will be resistance. Things will stir up. Your own household may get rattled. The spiritual realm is real, and when you go picking a fight, don't be surprised if something swings back.

Suit up. Ephesians 6 (*"Put on the full armor of God, so that you can take your stand against the devil's schemes" and following*) isn't fluff; it wasn't written for decoration. It's a war manual. Helmet, shield, sword, belt, boots, the full armor. This isn't a light show. It's combat.

He's the Deliverer, Not You

I'll say this again: This chapter isn't a guide. It's a testimony. It's a warning and a welcome.

There are amazing books and ministries dedicated to training people in this area—learn from them. Don't just wing it. The Bible says, *"My people perish for lack of knowledge."* (Hosea 4:6) And remember: You are not the hero in this story. You're just acting as the voice in the room, an ambassador of the Kingdom of Heaven. It's Jesus who sets people free. It's His name, His blood, His authority. Not yours. Not mine.

I've felt the surge of the Holy Spirit break through darkness like a thunderclap, and I've also felt the spiritual pushback when I got cocky or careless. This is serious. But it's also beautiful. There is nothing like watching someone walk out of a lifetime of torment into the light of freedom. Nothing like it. And I believe we'll see more and more of it in the days to come.

So again, I'm not an expert. But I am a witness. And I've learned this much:

Deliverance isn't about shaking or shouting or putting on a show.

It's about Jesus walking into a prison, driving away the ones who held you prisoner, turning the key to your cell and saying, *"Let's go. You're free now. Just don't go back."*

And if you're willing to pick up your mat, if you're ready to leave the grave behind,

He's more than ready to walk with you.

47

COMMUNITY

On the surface, this is a story about a boy with a troubled childhood who ran away, fell into a life of crime, incarceration, addiction, and then spun through those cycles until he was rescued and delivered by Jesus. Salvation, deliverance, redemption.

All that is true, but it misses an essential point that I need you to understand before we get to the final chapter.

This is the story of longsuffering.

That's a word we don't use much anymore, other words for it are "forbearance" or "patience."

Patience.

I am not a patient man.

But Lord, oh, Lord, people were so patient with me.

Bart. Betty. Dawn. Kevin. Travis. So many others.

When I was so hard to be patient with, these Christian brothers and sisters drew on strength that came not from themselves but from God, and they kept showing up. They could have given up, but instead they showed up.

That's what this takes – this broken, messy, dirty world filled with sin – for people to be drawn out of the kind of life I was in, it takes more than inviting someone to church or a Bible study and stopping there.

It takes a relentless pursuit of love.

That's in short supply, even among God's people, but if you catch anything from this story, it's that I would not be where I am without Jesus. True, without deliverance from my demons; true, without the Word of God; true, *but also* without a whole lot of people who were willing to walk alongside me.

It's essential that I get this point across; no matter who you are or where you are, we are all bound to fail if we don't have people walking alongside us. Maybe you're being pulled up, maybe you're pulling someone up, but if you're someone who identifies as a Christian, you are called to show up.

48

A NEW DAY

There's a quiet that lives in my mornings now. Before the house stirs and the noise of the day begins, I like to step outside with a cup of hot coffee and let the hush of rural Iowa wash over me. Judah, my dog, usually trots beside me. We don't say much, he doesn't speak, after all, but there's a friendship in his presence, in the way he lounges at my feet as if he knows we've both come a long way. The quiet of those morning moments reminds me that I'm not who I used to be. That the man I was – Kyle Orth – is gone.

Dead.

I say that without a shred of metaphor. Kyle Orth died. The man who manipulated, stole, abused, and used until there was nothing left? He's buried in a grave dug by God's grace and my repentance. What's left of that man are scars on others, memories that make my stomach turn, and the haunting truth that some people may never forgive me. And that's okay. I didn't earn forgiveness. I was handed it by God. And it's only through Him that I walk as Kyle *Hunter* now.

The name change didn't magically change my heart. Heart change came first, when I met Jesus in the middle of my destruction. But I chose to leave behind a name that carried too many wounds. Saul to Paul. Slave to free. Dead to alive.

Paul wrote in Galatians 2:20, *"I have been crucified with Christ and I no longer live, but Christ lives in me."* That verse is more than a poetic idea. It's the only explanation I have for what happened to me. Jesus killed Kyle Orth, and I buried him. We crucified the old self. And every day, I try to walk in my new self. Some days I do it well. Some days I struggle. But every day, I move forward.

Now, my life looks like something I never could've imagined from a jail cell or a trap house floor.

I'm a husband. Not perfect, but present. I love my wife deeply. She is my best friend, my partner, and my reminder that redemption shows up in the form of patience and grace. There's a warmth in our home now, one I never knew as a kid. I still catch myself marveling at the way she looks at me like I'm worth something. After all I've done? That's nothing short of a miracle!

I'm a father. A father to a little girl who lights up my world. I roughhouse with her, chase her giggles, and try to be the kind of dad who makes her feel safe, seen, and wildly loved. It stings that I don't have a relationship with my older daughter, Annie. That door remains closed, and I have to respect that. So I serve on the board of Kingdom Center, a ministry for youth – many of whom, like my first daughter, don't have dads around. I can't undo the pain I caused, but I can try to break the cycle for someone else.

I'm a landlord. A business leader. The general manager of a car dealership where I lead a growing team.

I'm also a community leader. I help lead the Good Friday Prayer Breakfast in Cedar Rapids. I volunteer with ministries like Hope CDA, where I sit with men who are still tangled in violence, addiction, and self-destruction, the same chains that nearly killed me. And I don't come at them from some pedestal. I sit eye to eye. I've *been* them. I still *fight* some of the same urges. The only difference is, I've learned to bring those urges to the cross every day and lay them down.

Jesus said in Luke 9:23, *"Whoever wants to be my disciple must deny themselves and take up their cross daily and follow me."* It's not a one-time decision. It's daily. Dying to myself isn't poetic, it's practical. Sometimes it means biting my tongue when I want to lash out. Sometimes it means staying up late to help a guy who's detoxing, even when I'm exhausted. Sometimes it means sitting with guilt for something I can't undo and praying to God to somehow use it.

There are people I've hurt who will never let me near their lives again, and I understand that. I respect it. But if you're one of those people reading this, I need you to hear me: From the bottom of my heart, I am sorry. It grieves me to my core to know how deeply I wounded others. I wish I could go back. I wish I could undo it all. But I can't.

So I do the next best thing. I try to live differently. Not for show, or recognition, or attention. But because I don't want to waste the grace I've been given. I try to give back what was so freely given to me. That's why I mentor men and speak to youth. That's why I pick up the phone at 2 a.m. when someone's spiraling. That's why I keep showing up, because God kept showing up for me, and He still does.

He will for you, too. Maybe your testimony has already proven it.

If my story (or yours) helps even one person who is drowning in addiction or the cycles of destructive thinking and living believe instead that change is possible, that God is real, that grace is enough – then revisiting all the pain through this book will be worth it.

I don't deserve the life I have. But I'm living it. And I'm not wasting it.

All the glory goes to God and the people He sent to help me find my way.

49

YOUR TURN

Okay, so now let's get into the nitty gritty. We've talked about where I came from, the hell I survived, and the mercy that pulled me out – but what about *you*?

What do you do if you're still in the pit? If you're reading this with an aching heart full of shame and your soul is just plain tired … this chapter is for you.

Let's not sugarcoat it: Turning your life around is *hard*. It's rough. It's not a TikTok transformation or some neat little three-step plan on a vision board. It's bloody, it's raw, and it begins in one place: The realization that your life is not your own.

"You are not your own; you were bought at a price. Therefore honor God with your bodies." (1 Corinthians 6:19-20)

That verse used to bother me. It sounded controlling. Like God wanted to take over. But now? Now I see it differently. It's not control; it's *rescue*. It's not domination, it's *deliverance*. You and I — we've both tried to run the show. And if you're anything like me, when you're in charge, you run it straight into the ground.

That realization is the turning point. Some short-lived emotional high is not the turning point. A motivational quote is not the turning point.

The turnaround starts when you finally come to the end of yourself and say:

"God, I give up. I can't do this anymore. I want You to be the Lord of my life. My life is now Yours."

That's surrender. And that's where the rebuilding begins.

I love how James opens his letter in the Bible:*"James, a bond-servant of God and of the Lord Jesus Christ."* (James 1:1)

Let that sink in for a second. James, who was Jesus' own brother, didn't name-drop. He didn't say, "James, sibling of the Messiah." He called himself a *bondservant*. You know what that means? It wasn't just a servant. A bondservant was a *willing slave*. Back then, if you were broke, starving, or desperate, you'd give yourself over to a landowner. In exchange for your service, he'd provide food, protection, and shelter. You didn't just work for him; you *belonged* to him.

That's what James was saying. "I belong to Jesus. He rescued me. I am His."

And friend, that's exactly what we need to do too.

Jesus doesn't just want your Sunday mornings. He wants your *life*. Not so He can boss you around, but so He can *restore* it. He wants to give you a new identity, a new way to walk, a new way to breathe.

But here's the next thing you need to understand: You are not meant to do this alone.

"Two are better than one....If either of them falls down, one can help the other up." (Ecclesiastes 4:9-10)

"Carry each other's burdens, and in this way you will fulfill the law of Christ." (Galatians 6:2)

We were created for *community*. I know you may not trust people. I didn't either. Maybe the people closest to you are the ones who hurt you the most. But isolation will *never* lead to transformation. Find a community of people who are following Jesus. They will not be perfect, but if you go looking, you'll find some who are following Him *sincerely*. Get around men or women who carry light, who speak life.

And listen, I can't stress this enough: FIND A MENTOR.

I don't care if you have to ask ten people, beg someone at church, or shoot your shot with the one person who seems like they've got their life together. Ask someone to pour into you. Buy them coffee. Ask questions. Be honest. Don't try to impress them, let them *help* you.

Get in your Bible. I know that reading can be hard – the Bible app on smart phones will read the Word to you. You don't have to read the whole thing cover to cover (but you could). You should probably not start at the beginning – the Old Testament is tricky, and we live in New Testament times. Start with the gospels: Matthew, Mark, Luke and John. Acts is great. Ephesians is great.

The Word of God is living and active, sharper than any double-edged sword. It will cut through the darkness, the troubles, and God will speak to you through the words. It is impossible to know God outside of His Word, the Bible.

Even reading a verse a day is good for your soul; a chapter a day is a great pace.

And above all … pray.
Pray like your life depends on it. Because it *does*.
There is no substitute. No shortcut. No app that can replace that genuine, desperate connection between you and your Creator.

Prayer isn't about fancy words. It's not a performance. Just talk to Him. Cry if you have to. Yell if you must. Whisper if that's all you've got in you. But *pray*. Over and over again. The power's not in how you say it, it's in *who you're saying it to*.

And lastly, take it slow.

Please don't try to fix everything at once. Don't panic about the job, the past, the addiction, the debt, the broken relationships. You didn't fall apart in a day, and you won't heal in one either.

Healing is not a sprint. It's a lifelong walk with Jesus.

So take a breath. One day at a time. One choice at a time. One moment at a time.

If you surrender your life to God…

If you turn away from sin and choose instead the things that give life …
If you get in the Word and pray, and keep praying…
If you find a mentor and build Christian community…
If you give yourself grace and take it slow…

I promise you – gradually, things will get better. I can't promise easy. I can't promise fast. But I *can* promise it's worth it.

"For there is now no condemnation for those who are in Christ Jesus," that's Romans 8:1.

That's the Bible, the promise of God.

I'm living proof.

If I can do it, you can too.

I promise.

50

TO THE ONES WHO LOVE AN ADDICT

This chapter is for you.

For the spouse who lies awake listening for a door to open or not open.

For the parent who picks up their phone with dread every time it buzzes.

For the child who learned early how to read moods, footsteps, silence.

For the sibling, the friend, the grandparent who keeps hoping this time will be different.

Loving an addict is one of the most emotionally complex callings a human heart can hold. It pulls you in opposite directions at once: Protect *and* confront. Hope *and* brace for impact. Love deeply while watching someone you love slowly unravel. It is exhausting. It is confusing. And it is not something you were ever trained for.

When I was in addiction, the people who helped me the most were not the ones who rescued me from consequences. They were the ones who loved me, prayed for me, told me the truth,

319

and connected me to professionals who knew how to handle something that love alone was not big enough to fix.

The least helpful people, even though they meant well, were the ones who gave me money, let me live with them while I was actively using, loaned me vehicles, or softened the fall-out of my decisions. Every softened consequence delayed the moment I had to face reality.

That may sound harsh. It is not meant to be. It is meant to be honest.

There are deep emotions involved here. Grief, fear, guilt, shame, anger, hope, despair. Watching someone you love who is going through a downward spiral is gut wrenching. It feels unnatural to step back when everything in you wants to step in. And because of that pain, loved ones often fall into one of two traps.

The first trap is begging and pampering.

This looks like pleading, reasoning, researching endlessly, chasing the perfect solution. There is often a fantasy hiding underneath it. If I just find the right program, the right doctor, the right words, the right environment, then this will be fixed. Love becomes frantic. Boundaries blur. And slowly, unintentionally, responsibility shifts from the addict to the people around them.

The second trap is threatening.

I will have you committed! I will kick you out! I will cut you off! I will disown you! These statements usually come from desperation, not cruelty. But threats that are fueled by emotion and not backed by consistent action lose their power quickly. Addiction does not respond to fear-based ultimatums. It learns how to wait them out.

Both traps have something in common. They place you at the center of a battle you cannot win.

Here is the truth that hurts before it heals. You can love someone unconditionally without shielding them from consequences. Addiction thrives when consequences are softened or removed. Love says, "I care about you." Enabling says, "I will protect you from the results of your choices." Those are not the same thing.

You cannot reason someone out of a behavior that is being driven by compulsion. Addiction hijacks logic, values, promises, and even faith language. Trying to reason with an addict produces circular arguments that go nowhere. Emotional bargaining goes nowhere. Ultimatums you cannot enforce weaken you and embolden the addiction.

What does help is calm, consistent response.

Not coldness. Not cruelty. Consistency.

Stay present, not permissive. Being emotionally available, listening, praying, encouraging healthy steps, and celebrating progress matter deeply.

Presence says, "You are not alone."

Permissiveness says, "This behavior is acceptable."

Holding the line between the two is one of the hardest but most loving things you could ever do.

You did not cause the addiction.

You cannot cure it.

You cannot control it.

Those truths are not failures. They are freedom.

What you can do is model stability, truth, faithfulness, and courage. Sometimes the strongest influence in an addict's life is not loud confrontation but quiet, steady integrity. A life that is anchored. A love that does not panic. A boundary that does not bend with every storm.

If the addict in your life is your child, unity matters. You and your spouse must be on the same page. Addiction will exploit division quickly. Mixed messages confuse everyone and help no one. Loving your child well means agreeing together on boundaries and support, even when it breaks your heart.

And this part matters more than most people realize. The best way you can help is to get them support, real support. They need professionals, community, accountability, and structure. They need people who are not emotionally entangled in every decision. You are too close to be the sole lifeline. That does not mean you stop loving. It means you stop trying to be the solution.

Enabling is trying to save someone and solve their problems.

Helping is getting them connected to people and systems that can actually support change.

As Christians, we sometimes confuse love with permissiveness. We mistake compassion for rescuing. But we cannot save anyone. Salvation, healing, and transformation are a co-laboring between the individual and God. We can walk alongside. We can pray. We can share the truth. But we cannot replace conviction, repentance, or surrender.

Loving an addict will cost you something. It will require restraint when you want to rush in. Courage when you want to avoid conflict. Faith when outcomes are uncertain. But loving well does not mean losing yourself, your peace, or your integrity.

You are allowed to be whole while they are still broken.

You are allowed to set boundaries and still love deeply.

You are allowed to trust God with what you cannot fix.

This road is often long. Progress is rarely linear. But steady love, clear boundaries, prayer, and appropriate support create the environment for addiction to finally be overcome and a new life of freedom to begin.

51

AND THE GREATEST OF THESE IS LOVE

The sun dipped low behind the Iowa fields, golden over the land. The light, soft and sacred, filtered through the trees like grace. It reminded me of something I once read: *"Above all, put on love, which binds everything together in perfect harmony."* (Colossians 3:14)

After everything, after the brokenness, the prison bars, the betrayals, the victories, the healings, the deliverance, the restoration, the fatherhood, the ministry, the calling … after all of it … there is still one thing that matters more than anything else.

Love.

Not the watered-down, packaged-up Hallmark version. Not the conditional, transactional, performance-based kind. Not the imposter, that lusty thing that draws us in, disappoints and disappears. I'm talking about *real* love, the kind that bled on a cross. The kind that forgives. The kind that stays when it would be easier to walk away. The kind that transforms addicts into sons, convicts into kings, orphans into heirs.

I once thought my story was about survival. Then I thought it was about redemption. But I've come to realize it was always about love.

You can memorize all the verses, clean up your life, pay your tithes, preach in prisons, and write books about your testimony, but if it isn't rooted in love, it's all noise. Just a clanging cymbal. Paul said it best in 1 Corinthians 13:

> *"If I speak in the tongues of men or of angels, but do not have love, I am only a resounding gong or a clanging cymbal….If I have a faith that can move mountains, but do not have love, I am nothing."*

Nothing. That's what I was without love. Even on my best days.

It starts with loving God. Not just believing in Him, not just obeying Him, not just asking Him to bless your plans, but loving Him. *All in.* No prenup. No backup plan. No halfway.

> *Jesus said, "You shall love the Lord your God with all your heart, all your soul, all your mind, and all your strength." (Mark 12:30)*

It's not a polite suggestion. It's the greatest commandment.

And here's the thing: I've learned you can't really love others well until you get this one right. You'll end up trying to love people from your wounds instead of being able to love them from a place of your healing. True love doesn't flow from fear, it flows out of your faith. Until you're loving from a place of interconnectedness with Jesus, you'll put expectations on yourself and the other person that only God was meant to carry.

But when you love Jesus, truly love Him, it changes *everything*.

Your heart gets softer. Your ego gets smaller. Your priorities shift. You stop needing to be the hero. And you start living to serve.

I've seen the power of this firsthand. In the way my wife still chooses me, even when I'm hard to love. In the way my daughter reaches for me with eyes that have never seen my past, only my present. I've seen it in the way that men who were once my rivals or enemies now stand beside me as brothers. In the way the Spirit moves when we gather to pray, not with eloquent words, but with genuine love for God and one another.

Love restores what shame destroyed.

Love breaks generational curses that trauma tried to pass on to the next.

Love builds bridges over gaps we thought were too wide to cross.

Love isn't weak. Love is the strongest thing in the universe. That's why the enemy fights it so hard. That's why bitterness, pride, and division are so seductive, they're counterfeit comforts.

But God *is* love.

Not God *has* love. Not God *gives* love. God *is* love.

So when you make your life about love, you're making your life about God. And that's the only thing worth building your legacy on.

Here's how I want to be remembered:

Not for what I escaped, but for how I loved.

Not for the size of my platform, but for the size of my heart.

Not for the empire I built, but for the people I laid my life down for.

Because love looks like something. It looks like dishes washed when no one's watching. Like showing up to meetings no one thanks you for. Like forgiving when there's no apology. Like holding your tongue when you want to be right. Like blessing your enemies. Praying for them. Like sacrificing your comfort. Like opening your home. Like telling someone the truth when it would be easier to flatter them.

Love is inconvenient. It costs you everything. But it gives you more than you ever had to begin with.

So here's my final word. My altar call. My invitation to you, friend, wherever you've been.

Love God with *everything*.

Not just when the worship is good or the sermon hits home or life is going your way. Love Him when you're in a dry spell. Love Him when you're at your lowest. Love Him when it hurts. Love Him when you're confused. Love Him when you're winning. Love Him when you're not.

And He will love you back. It's who He is, it's what He does.

Then from that love, let love pour out to everyone around you: your family, your neighbors, your enemies, the broken, the overlooked, the difficult.

Radical love isn't optional for Christians. It's the mark of a true disciple. Jesus said, *"By this everyone will know that you are my disciples, if you love one another."* (John 13:35)

This is the most excellent way.

This is the only thing that will matter when your earthly light goes out and eternity begins.

This is the heartbeat of Heaven and the anthem of every story that's ever been redeemed.

Love.

You can't fake it, can't brand it.

This love comes from a man who stretched out His arms and said, *"I love you this much."*

And then died to prove it.

That's the love I'm chasing.

And I hope you'll chase it too.

EPILOGUE

If you've made it this far, I want you to know something important: This story is not about how broken I was, and it's not about how strong I became. It's about community. It's about people who showed up when it was inconvenient, uncomfortable, and costly. People who didn't just talk about love but practiced it. People who became the hands and feet of Jesus in very real, very practical ways.

My life did not change because of a single moment, a perfect prayer, or a sudden flash of clarity. It changed because people stepped into the mess with me. They prayed when I couldn't. They told me the truth when it would have been easier to stay quiet. They refused to enable me, but they also refused to abandon me. They sat across tables, opened their homes, made phone calls, connected me with professionals, and walked with me one step at a time. That kind of love is not flashy. It's slow. It's persistent. And it's powerful.

This book exists the same way my healing did: through community. Writing it was not a solo act. It was not a display of how smart I am or how well I can tell a story. It was a picture of grace. Editors, filmmakers, friends, mentors, and encouragers all leaned in. Beautiful, thoughtful, loving people gave their time, their gifts, and their wisdom to help tell this story honestly. In many ways, putting this together mirrored my actual journey. It took a village. It took patience. It took truth. And it took grace.

This story began as a film, and as I write this, that film is in its final stages. Somewhere along the way, it also became a book, and it will likely become another one after this. I don't know exactly what's next. Maybe this leads to speaking opportunities. Maybe it opens doors I can't see yet. Maybe it simply lands in the hands of someone who needs hope at just the right moment. I'm content not knowing. I'll leave the outcomes to God.

What I do know is this: I am deeply grateful. Grateful for how far God has brought me. Grateful for the people He used along the way. Grateful that my story is no longer defined by my worst decisions, but by the grace that met me there. If this book proves anything, I hope it proves that no one gets free alone, and no one is too far gone to be reached by love.

This is not my victory story. It's ours.

The story doesn't end here.

The conversation continues at KillingKyleOrth.com.

You'll find helpful resources and you can join our community there.

If this book has been helpful to you,

would you please let others know about it?

Post about it on social media.

Interview Kyle on your blog, podcast or publication.

We would love your honest review at Amazon or Goodreads.

Your review does so much to help others find this book!

Just search Killing Kyle Orth wherever books are sold and click on reviews to add yours.

Thank you very much!

Bulk pricing for this book is available for organizations, ministries and groups.

To book Kyle to speak at your church, organization or conference, visit KillingKyleOrth.com.

You can also connect with Killing Kyle Orth on Facebook and Instagram.

KillingKyleOrth.com | FascinationFilms.com | AcornsAndOaks.com

Special thanks to Michelle Hill at Winning Proof for her consultation and partnership in the publication of this book: WinningProof.com.

www.ingramcontent.com/pod-product-compliance
Lightning Source LLC
Chambersburg PA
CBHW041302120726
48005CB00014B/1836